Making an
After Dinner Speech

Making an
After Dinner Speech

*How to make a speech that has
them rolling in the aisles*

JOHN BOWDEN

2nd Edition

How To Books

This book is dedicated to my mother Babs,
who knows all my jokes backwards and
frequently tells them that way.

Published in 2000 by
How To Books Ltd, 3 Newtec Place,
Magdalen Road, Oxford OX4 1RE, United Kingdom.
Tel: (01865) 793806. Fax: (01865) 248780.
email: info@howtobooks.co.uk
http://www.howtobooks.co.uk

First edition 1999
Second edition 2000

British Library Cataloguing in Publication Data
A catalogue record for this book is available from
the British Library

Cartoons by Mike Flanagan
Cover design by Shireen Nathoo Design
Cover image by PhotoDisc

Produced for How To Books by Deer Park Productions
Typeset by Kestrel Data, Exeter
Printed and bound by Cromwell Press Ltd, Trowbridge, Wiltshire

NOTE: The material contained in this book is set out in good
faith for general guidance and no liability can be accepted
for loss or expense incurred as a result of relying in particular
circumstances on statements made in the book. Laws and
regulations are complex and liable to change, and readers should
check the current position with the relevant authorities before
making personal arrangements.

Contents

List of illustrations

Preface
to the Second Edition

The posh frocks are coming out of mothballs and ample physiques are valiantly squeezing into dinner jackets. The annual dinner season is once again upon us and all around the country men and women are busily writing and rehearsing their speeches.

An after dinner speech should be light-hearted, humorous and friendly. It should not deal with 'big' issues. I have therefore avoided the touchingly sentimental and profound and instead concentrated on the frivolous, off-beat and entertaining. The trick is to construct a tailor-made script that has the *appearance* of being nothing more than a spontaneous chat with friends. This handbook will show you how to prepare and present a speech that packs a punch, that has real impact. Impact is the sizzle in the sausage.

There's an awful lot of people out there who have had funny or strange experiences. Has something quirky ever happened to you? If you have a story or convincing tale to tell, then why not spin the yarn at your club or company dinner? You could even earn money by getting yourself on the after dinner speaking circuit. You don't need to be famous. Agencies are always on the look-out for 'new talent'. Audiences simply want to hear something *different, unusual* and *interesting*. Most of all, they want to be *entertained*.

Heard the one about the writer who used masculine nouns and pronouns throughout his book? This stems from my desire to avoid ugly, cumbersome English. No discrimination, prejudice or bias is intended. This book really is written for *everyone* who wants to make speeches which are relevant, topical, fast, punchy, funny – and downright impressive. Women and men should have an equal right to buy it!

John Bowden

Acknowledgements

Many people assisted in the production of this book and I am grateful to them all. Below I have singled out a few to whom I would like to show my particular appreciation.

First, special thanks are due to Ivor Spencer, the only Toastmaster to have officiated at over 1,000 Royal events worldwide. The Prince of Toastmasters has introduced celebrities for 40 years and has listened to over 50,000 after dinner speeches. Quite simply, his experience is unrivalled – as is his advice.

Thanks also to Gyles Brandreth, a former After Dinner Speaker of the Year, for his kind permission to reproduce numerous tips and anecdotes from his entertaining autobiography *Under the Jumper*.

I would particularly like to thank the directors of Celebrity Speakers Limited, an international speaker bureau, who provided an invaluable collective view on the four essential ingredients needed to make an effective after dinner speech.

I am also greatly indebted to each of the following speakers for revealing their personal recipes for blending those ingredients to create the perfect after dinner speech: Tony Ball, Tony Benn MP, Dickie Bird, Heather Couper, Lord Cowdrey of Tonbridge, Sir Ranulph Fiennes, Teresa Gorman MP, Sir John Harvey-Jones, Rachel Heyhoe Flint, Lord Janner of Braunstone, Charles Kennedy MP, Ian McCaskill, Professor Patrick Minford, Professor Laurie Taylor, Harvey Thomas, Barry Took and Sir Peter Ustinov.

Finally, thanks are due to Alan Litten, a professional colleague, for reading the draft manuscript and identifying 'soft' and confusing areas that needed expansion or fine-tuning. Alan's judgement and advice is always an asset.

1

Making it Entertaining

The basic purpose of an after dinner speech is to entertain. While the occasional injection of a serious note can sometimes serve as a much-needed anchor, the seriousness should never be allowed to predominate. You want your speech to come over as a light and amusing social chat with friends.

You can ensure your speech remains upbeat, chatty and highly entertaining throughout by:

- Making happy talk.

- Knowing your audience.

- Developing your theme.

- Jump starting your creativity.

Let's consider each in turn.

MAKING HAPPY TALK

The moment you rise to address an audience, you also step onto a stage. When you open your mouth to speak, you enter show business. The more you accept that, the more successful you will be. Your audience are not gathered to learn or be convinced: they're sitting there to have a good time. Don't disappoint them. Your overall aim is to leave your audience feeling happier during and after your speech than they were before it.

An after dinner speech should be:

- optimistic

- uncomplicated

- enlivened with humour.

Optimistic

This is not the time to share your personal woes, paint a gloomy picture of the present or offer dire predictions about the future. You are not there to instruct or persuade. Keep the overall tone light and upbeat. Give them what they want to hear and what the occasion requires.

Uncomplicated

Don't make your audience strain to get your point. Develop your speech around a central theme and one or two simple, straightforward points that they can easily grasp.

Enlivened with humour

Audiences want to get away from all that serious stuff that dominates their everyday lives and just have a good laugh. They have come to be entertained.

KNOWING YOUR AUDIENCE

What do all after dinner **speakers** have in common? They have to have an audience. They must address *people*. And what do all successful after dinner **speeches** have in common? They are *partnerships* between the speaker and the audience.

As a speaker, you have to acknowledge the audience's importance and include them. You really have no choice. If you ignore them, they won't be entertained. If they're not entertained, your speech will have failed. A speaker *needs* the attention of his audience. They *have* to listen, and their laughter *has* to be spontaneous, otherwise it's worthless.

A prospector does not go out and simply start drilling holes randomly in the hope that one of them will hit the spot. No, he knows the earth will be the source of his eventual wealth, but first he must do his groundwork. He must discover where oil is likely to be found, and only then will he drill to produce that gusher. In the same way, a speaker must regard his audience as the source that will supply *his* reward. But first he must study them to find out where most mirth is likely to be mined.

Thinking audience

The key to good after dinner speaking is to **think audience**. Always remember that there is only one ultimate judge of the effectiveness of a speech and that is the audience. The audience is supreme.

The material you use will depend upon the character of your fellow diners – youth club, students, businesspeople, church members, old soldiers, sportspeople or whatever. Revellers at a stag party won't be entertained by the same material as a matinee of senior citizens. Teenagers go for zany, madcap jokes. Old folks prefer slower, broad anecdotal humour. Audiences in their twenties appreciate speed, wit and sophistication. Thirty-, forty- and fifty-somethings prefer a little 'adult humour'.

Generalisations? Of course. But teenagers won't laugh at the same material as their parents. Each generation has a different outlook and sense of humour. Don't just play to your own age.

Know more about your audience than you need to know. The more information you have in reserve, the more selective you can be about what you choose to say and how you choose to say it. Understanding what people want to hear means listening more than speaking. An architect cannot build you a house unless he knows where you want to live. Your hairdresser cannot give you a good haircut, unless you have told him how you want to look when he's finished. You cannot tell people what they want to hear, unless you have found out first.

DEVELOPING YOUR THEME

A speech without a **theme** is like a car without an engine: the only way it can go is downhill. You must have a proposition, a single dominant idea running throughout. Choose a clear, central theme that suits the occasion and audience. Go for one that's novel, provocative and original – but don't overdo it – you want to entertain, not shock.

Slant your theme to suit your audience. You need to find one which this particular audience will identify with and find relevant and interesting. Your theme must be general enough to fit the alloted time, but specific enough to be meaningful to your audience.

Too wide	Just right	Too narrow
Rugby	Our latest tour of Scotland	The game against Oban
Golf	The forthcoming season	Nick's hole-in-one
XYZ Ltd	A review of the year	The chairman's new desk
I.T.	A parody of conference buzzwords	My ThinkPad

All your intimate confessions, witty observations, perceptive one-liners, amusing anecdotes and hilarious insights into the state of the world must then be appropriate to this core theme. Secondary points should be made only if they do not detract from your primary message.

Keeping them in the picture
Keep the group attitude in mind throughout and personalise even the most remote issue so they can see a connection between themselves and it. If people can see how your subject matter relates to them, they will remain interested.

JUMP STARTING YOUR CREATIVITY

Visualise a person being creative. Put the book down for a few moments and imagine someone actually *creating* something. What did you see? The odds are that you saw an inventor, a painter, a musician, a scientist, or some other specialist producing an important new product, a piece of art or a scientific finding. Of course all these people were being creative, but the view that creativity must involve great achievements is far too narrow. Why did you not see an *ordinary* person – perhaps yourself – making something or solving some problem – or creating an after dinner speech? As the American psychologist, Abraham Maslow put it: 'A first-rate soup is more creative than a second-rate painting.'

Creativity is *not* confined to the gifted few; creative people are not a race apart. Nor are they necessarily particularly clever. Albert Einstein had to spend an extra year in high school before being accepted by the Zurich Polytechnic School and, when he left, they would not recommend him for a job; F. Scott Fitzgerald may have penned *The Great Gatsby*, but he was anything but a great speller; and Charles Darwin would not have survived even the most basic test of numeracy.

Getting great ideas

Have you ever gone to bed totally stumped for a solution to some problem, and woken up the next morning with an inspired answer? The same trick can come to your aid in preparing a speech. But first it is essential to know precisely what you want to achieve. Chance favours the prepared mind. Serendipity has to be earned. It is no substitute for hard work; it is a bonus to it.

Putting the matter to the back of your mind triggers that marvellous part of the brain where the subconscious dwells. By concentrating your thoughts on possible ways you could structure your speech and express yourself, you are also awakening your instinctive ability to recognise the best methods. The creative process can take place during all those times of the day when you are occupied by the most prosaic matters – shopping, watching TV, mowing the lawn. So *always* carry a notebook and pen.

Keeping an open mind

Allow your subconscious mind to take over; let your critical facility relax. As ideas come to you, do not immediately accept the first or most obvious stories, gags and thoughts. Look for alternatives. Do not set too high a standard in the early stages, and do not reject anything too quickly. Make it a habit to search for a little longer and to dig just a little deeper. The subconscious is shy, elusive and unwieldy, but it *is* possible to learn to tap it and even direct it.

A brain of two halves

Much research has gone into the workings of the human brain. An over-simplistic, yet useful model of the brain is one of a cortex divided into halves, or hemispheres, each being good at different things. The left half is logical and a little boring; the right is creative and exciting.

You must learn how to turn off your left mode of thinking, and turn on your right mode of thinking. One deceptively simple way to do this is to think about your speech while you are engaged in some physical activity, such as jogging; or while you are feeling very relaxed, perhaps in the bath, in the local, or immediately before or after sleep. Another method is to give your brain a task which the left hemisphere *cannot* – or *will not* – handle, such as making sense of abstract lines and shapes. It will reject the task and the imaginative right hemisphere will accept the challenge instead.

It is easy to recognise when you are engaged in right mode thinking. Time will seem to fly by. You will be:

- almost unaware of what would normally be considered distractions

- active yet very calm

- thinking in images, not words

- engrossed in the task.

Creative ideas do not come to the half-hearted. The stereotype of the absent-minded professor, so absorbed in his thoughts that he fumbles through the routine tasks of everyday life, is an amusing yet essentially accurate picture of right mode thinking in action.

So don't put off contemplating until the last minute. Ponder as you wander. Chew over your ideas as you eat. Think as you drink. And sleep on it. Ideas are like beanshoots – they grow in the dark. Every pensive reflection will pay dividends when the time comes to collect your thoughts and say them out loud to your audience.

QUESTIONS AND ANSWERS

What is the ideal size for an after dinner audience?
That depends on a number of factors, not least the character and personality of the speaker. Many people find it awkward to address audiences of fewer than about 30 and difficult to communicate effectively with audiences of over about 150.

Do the people know each other – and you? A friendly coach party of 60 who all know each other is easier to play to than an audience comprised of 30 separate couples or – worse still – 60 individual guests. The venue affects things too. Sixty people in a room above a pub may be an ideal-sized audience, while the same number would be embarassingly small in most banqueting halls.

The great paradox of audiences is that the larger they are the more they become one person. Instead of becoming more diverse they become more homogeneous. It is therefore easier to reinforce group unity with a large audience. But if the number approaches 200 any genuine intimacy will become very difficult to achieve. You need to become an orator rather than a speaker.

The consensus therefore seems to be that the optimum number lies somewhere between 60 and 150.

I intend to include a serious idea in my speech. Any suggestions about how I can do this and still keep my talk entertaining?
A speech that is all fluff can sometimes become tiresome and vacuous. Something of greater weight, such as a serious statement of loyalty for the group or organisation you are addressing, can be useful. But don't overdo it; the audience wants to be entertained. Leave your soapbox at home.

Funnily enough, a serious point sandwiched between two slices of thought-provoking humour can be very effective:

Humour: A lorry got stuck under (local) bridge, a crowd gathered but no one knew what to do. Some said tear the top off the lorry, others said dismantle the bridge. The argument raged on – top off the lorry, dismantle the bridge. Finally, a small child at the back asked, 'Why don't you let the air out of the tyres?'

Seriousness: Even the most experienced panel of experts can miss the answer to a professional problem precisely because they *are* experienced. We need to be able to step back and be more alert to the existence of alternative, often simpler approaches and solutions.

Humour: Like the electrician who was examining a refrigerator that was using too much electricity. He tried all the usual tests and checks but couldn't find the reason. Then he stepped back – as it were – and asked himself why the kitchen was so cold. 'How do you get the room so cool?' he asked. And the lady of the house replied, 'I just keep the door of the fridge wide open all day.'

Can you suggest any other way that I can improve my creativity?
The next time you are facing a problem with your speech, throw in a bunch of bananas! Open a dictionary randomly, turn away and point to a word – perhaps *banana*. This word will release you from your current dominant – and possibly unimaginative – mind-set.

Say you are looking for a good line to round off a speech about green issues – without success. You throw in the word *triangle*. Does that help? Not really. How many sides does one have? Three. Still no joy. What is it? It's a shape – ahah! That can also mean the condition something's in. So how about a little play on words?

'Good planets are hard to find . . . let's try to keep ours in decent shape.'

Things won't always work out quite as neatly or easily as that. But a bunch of bananas will *always* allow you to step back and consider a problem from a fresh and unusual perspective. And it will increase your vocabulary!

SUMMARY

- Your overall aim is to leave your audience feeling happier during and after your speech than they were before it.
- It should be optimistic, uncomplicated and enlivened with humour.
- Always 'think audience'.
- Choose a theme that is tailor-made for this audience.
- Jump start your creativity.
- Start thinking about your speech today.

2

Choosing the Right Material

A good after dinner speech includes an entertaining balance of humorous one-liners, longer stories, and friendly mickey taking – all possibly underpinned by one or two more serious thoughts. To be interesting, entertaining and memorable your material needs to be *meaningful* to the audience. They must *identify* with your words and sentiments.

The material you choose must be right for *this* audience, for *this* occasion – and for you. A firm's annual dinner will give you the chance to make a few humorous remarks about a rival's lousy products; at a football club dance you could kick off with some soccer stories.

From the moment you begin to speak the audience is asking itself: 'Is this speech for me?' This gives you a wonderful opportunity to get in quickly with the right answer. Within 30 seconds the audience should be telling itself: 'Yes, this speech *is* for me! It's relevant, original, topical . . . What's more, it's fun!'

This chapter will consider how you should go about selecting and devising good, relevant material for your speech. In particular it will discuss the importance of:

- Finding anecdotes and jokes.
- Inventing jokes.
- Switching jokes.
- Quoting people.

FINDING ANECDOTES AND JOKES

The vital thing with a tight-knit group is to establish yourself immediately as an insider, to make references only they will understand, so that right from your first few sentences they feel that you are one of them – whether you are or not. An audience will always enjoy a speech more if they are made a part of it. Here

are a few ways to convince people that you have a real understanding of their specialised world.

Telling them what they want to hear
Think audience and think **theme**. There's nothing wrong with
preaching to the converted. Audiences *like* to be told things
they already know and they *love* to hear opinions with which they
concur.

If you want to ingratiate yourself with an audience – and you
should want to – use *your* humour to reinforce *their* views. If they
believe strongly in green issues, then you might remark: 'If you
take a bath in this city, the water leaves a ring around *you*.'

Telling meaningful stories
Everyone loves a story. If you can find a relevant anecdote or gag
you are onto a winner. Matching your choice of anecdotes and
jokes to the nature of the audience is easy when the group is
homogeneous – medical stories for doctors, religious anecdotes
for the clergy, horsey tales for the gymkhana club.

If you are addressing an audience of fishermen in Scotland, they
will not warm to a story set in a gay disco in San Francisco. In
contrast, if you are speaking to an audience of amateur cricketers,
a blow-by-blow account of a number 11 batsman's final over
heroics is sure to bowl them over.

Knowing their history
A few references to the history of this illustrious company,
club or society are sure to go down well. However, make
sure you get your facts right. *Cave anorakem* (beware of the
anorak).

Using your local knowledge
What are the locals currently complaining about? Maybe the
traffic wardens are being a little over-zealous in the city centre.
Perhaps the Mormons have just hit town. Whatever the perceived
problem, reverse it, and consider including it as a 'funny thing
happened to me' line.

'A funny thing happened to me on the way here this evening . . .'

'–the traffic lights were working in Queen's Street.'

'–I didn't see a fight outside the King's Head.'

'–my train was on time.'

Exploiting their irritations

Every organisation has one current overriding collective gripe. Exploit it.

'The trouble with (their current Mr Nasty) is that he is suffering from paralysis of the intellect.'

'(Mr Nasty) is the kind of man who would cut down a 200-year-old oak and mount the stump to make a speech on conservation.'

'I hear they're erecting a huge statue of (Mr Nasty) in Trafalgar Square. They are doing it so the pigeons can express the views of all of us.'

Focusing on shared experiences

Talk about experiences that you shared with the audience. Relate anecdotes that help the audience tap into common events.

'Didn't we have a blooming good time on our visit to the Chelsea Flower Show . . . ?'

Fostering group spirit

Your aim should be to create social cohesion and good feelings. Make your audience feel proud to work for *this* company, to be involved in *this* sales launch, to be a member of *this* golf club. Remind them of the values and experiences they share. Concentrate on whatever it is that binds them together.

Bob Monkhouse began an after dinner speech to an audience of 100 grocers and their partners by observing that:

'You do look well. It's reassuring to look round me and see how healthy 200 people can be despite living off a diet made up exclusively of food that's past its sell-by date.'

Through this apparent revelation, each grocer and partner discovered that everyone around them ate out-dated food too. They were no longer alone. He had shown them they they were members of a special group. He had fostered a genuine group spirit.

Being topical

You win Brownie points for topicality. A story based on – or even just referring to – a current event, news item or piece of local gossip will tell them this speech was written specifically for them, because an identical one could not possibly have been delivered before.

In the following example, the speaker makes a reference to today's football result before going on to tell a previously scripted gag. This simple device leaves the audience with the impression that the gag is topical too:

> 'So poor old Melchester Rovers got hammered again this after-noon . . . Their manager (or name him) won't stand for any nonsense though. At half time he caught a couple of fans climbing over the stadium wall. He was furious. He grabbed them by the collars and said, "Now you just get back in there and watch the game till it finishes!" '

What an audience knows is a dynamic thing. It's constantly changing. New information becomes available, and old infor-mation becomes tired and fades away. Today's hot topic is tomorrow's yesterday's news. How can you know your audience's current knowledge of events? A few enquiries may help, but it often comes down to a gut feeling and to common sense. A big story that broke yesterday is safe, a lesser story that broke within the last hour isn't.

Picking up buzz words

A two-day sales conference can be hard graft for all those in-volved. At dinner, they want to get away from everything they have been taught and yet be able to have a laugh at it. The trick here is to pick up the current buzz word – say, *Motivation 2000* – and weave a few lines around it:

> 'First it was Save the Birmingham Six, then Free the Guildford Four, and even Liberate the Weatherfield One. Now they im-plore us: Release the Motivation 2000.'

Using whatever works

Everything 'new' is derivative to a certain extent. Paradoxically, if you can find, adapt and personalise some 'old' material to make it relevant and meaningful to an audience, you are being highly creative and original. The following anecdote was heard recently at a football club's end-of-season dinner:

> 'Kevin's a generous manager. He took the whole team out for a slap-up meal. The boss told the waiter that he'd have steak and kidney pie. "And the vegetables?" the waiter asked. 'Oh, they'll have the same," Kevin said.'

This leaders-and-led story went down well – not least amongst the vegetables. No one seemed to recall a very similar tale being told about Margaret Thatcher and her Cabinet in the mid-1980s. The speaker had found an almost perfect fit and made a few minor adjustments. You can do the same. Just try to look through potential source material with a fresh eye.

If you find a story about Florence Nightingale that could help expound your theme, make a few embellishments here and there and allow your society treasurer to play the role of the Lady of the Lamp. If you find an ideal line by Mark Twain, put it in the mouth of your company chairman. Don't allow the facts to spoil a good story. As Woody Allen didn't say, 'Your aim is to be entertaining, not necessarily accurate.'

INVENTING JOKES

A joke is magical; a grain of truth grown to grotesque proportions turning on an absurdity of life or language. It may be zany, bizarre, nonsensical, but in its own way it has a point of view. It may be exaggerated, distorted, paradoxical, but it can always be reduced to a certain logic.

You need a starting point, so think audience – and think theme. The starting point for each gag is: 'What do I want this to say?' The answer to that question doesn't have to be funny. The joke that you create will be. Jokes can be used to say something quite serious in a funny way. If you wanted to share your thoughts on the fundamental difference between capitalism and communism, you might say:

'Under capitalism, it's dog eat dog. Under communism, it's just the opposite.'

Or maybe you want to give them your vision of the year 2084. In which case, you might ponder:

'The factory of the future will have only two employees – a man and a dog. The man will be there to feed the dog. The dog will be there to stop the man from touching the equipment.'

Constructing a joke
Every joke you hear has been 'built' by someone. And that person had exactly the same materials as you have now. Let's see how you can use those raw materials to create customised comedy.

'Our local vet and taxidermist have merged with the slogan: "Either way you get your dog back." '

Why is this funny? Because of its construction. Set-up . . . sting. Re-phrase the same idea and it falls apart. If the line had been:

'You are sure to get your dog back now whatever the outcome of the operation because our local vet and taxidermist have joined forces.'

the comedy is lost. The joke is too cumbersome and the set-up and tagline have been reversed.

A good way to kick-start your comic creativity is to *begin* with a punch line and then *work back* to create the set-up! Let me explain. Say you want to devise a few jokes on the theme of crime and punishment. You begin by thinking about cops and robbers. What do they do? Cops look for *leads, nick* people and ask people to *accompany* them to the station. Robbers get *charged, let off* or *put away*. Then you ask yourself whether any of the key words you have come up with have other meanings which could serve as joke set-ups. Dogs have leads; razor blades nick you; singers are accompanied by pianos. So you might come up with the following:

'A man broke into Battersea Dogs Home and stole all the animals. None of the dogs have been recovered but the police say they've got plenty of leads.'

'A burglar broke into a razor blade factory . . . he got nicked.'

'A man was caught breaking into a piano factory . . . he was asked to accompany the police to the station.'

'A man broke into a power station while his mate broke into a fireworks factory. The first man got charged, the second got let off.'

'A thief broke into a storage container factory . . . he got put away.'

Types of jokes

Most gags come under one – or occasionally more than one – of the following categories. Let's take the theme of doctors and nurses to illustrate them. The techniques employed in fashioning each form of frivolity are usually self-evident, although a few words of explanation have been added, where necessary:

- **Exaggeration.** He's never had a day's sickness in his life. He always makes it last at least three months.
- **The insult.** She's a lousy nurse. She couldn't even put a dressing on a salad.
- **Illogical logic.** I went to the doctor's this morning. I couldn't go last week – I was sick.
- **The pun.** A paediatrician is a man with little patients.
- **Word play** (not to be confused with puns). I told my doctor that my irregular heartbeat was bothering me. He said, 'Don't worry. We'll soon put a stop to it.'
- **The picture** (the gag creates a mental picture). No nurse, I said prick his boil!
- **The reverse.** A man walks into a doctor's surgery with a duck on his head. The doctor says, 'What can I do for you?' And the duck replies, 'I want this wart on my foot removed.'
- **The twisted cliché.** An apple a day keeps the doctor away . . . and so does living in the wrong postal code area.
- **Truthfulness.** A specialist is a doctor with a smaller practice but a bigger home.

SWITCHING JOKES

So far we've stressed the importance of choosing the right sort of material for your speech and discussed ways you can devise your own jokes. Now let's talk about **switching** gags. What you have to do is take the *idea* behind a funny but as yet unrelated gag and then transfer it to the subject and theme of your speech.

Say you need some golfing gags. Here are half-a-dozen examples of how jokes on a variety of topics can be switched to meet your needs.

1. 'When we were in the National Gallery, I overheard this elderly man ask his wife what she thought of the Picasso exhibition. "It's not bad," she said, "but I prefer art." '
Switch: 'I once played 18 holes with Nick Faldo at St Andrews. As the round ended, I asked timidly, "What do you think of my game?" And Faldo said, "Not bad, but I still prefer golf." '

2. 'When I asked Dave why he was so relaxed about his overdraft, he said: "Because it's grown big enough to look after itself." '
Switch: 'I'm not in the *least* worried about my handicap. Believe me, it's big enough to look after itself.'

3. 'This little old lady down the Post Office asked me how to do the National Lottery. It was a double rollover week and she'd decided to have a flutter for the very first time. So I showed her. "But how do you know *which* six numbers will win?" she asked.'
Switch: 'Then there was this sweet young thing who was being initiated into the mysteries of the glorious game by her boyfriend. "And now tell me," she said coyly, "*which* club do I use to make a hole-in-one?" '

4. 'An ancient philosopher once told his young pupil, "Together, we shall explore the meaning of life and unravel the mysteries of the universe." The pupil looked up at his mentor and said, "Great . . . and what are we going to do tomorrow?" '
Switch: 'Two women approached (club professional) in the club shop. "Do you wish to learn to play golf, madam?" he asked one. "Oh no," she said, "it's my friend who wants to learn. I learnt yesterday." '

5. 'That man is so fat he has to look in a mirror to find out what colour socks he's got on.'

Switch: ' "When I put the ball where I can reach it," said the portly golfer, "I can't see it, and when I put it where I can see it I can't reach it." '

6. 'Bart began to enter the details required on the front of his examination paper. But he couldn't remember the number of the exam centre, and he didn't know the centre's reference number, the exam code, or even the date. In frustration, he turned to his neighbour and exclaimed, "This is a difficult exam, isn't it?" '

Switch: 'A guest on (local) golf course placed the ball in position, swung and missed it three times, hit it the fourth time, and then turned to his host and said, "This is a difficult course, isn't it?" '

QUOTING PEOPLE

An apt and amusing quotation can really lift a speech and you'll find a wide selection in Appendix 4, towards the end of the book. But don't overdo it. Quoting people can sound pompous. Just give one or two appropriate lines and do it in a very casual way. If you are quoting someone famous, either make it clear you had to look it up or give the impression you're not absolutely sure of your source:

'I am reminded of the words of Groucho Marx – reminded I should say by my wife, who looked them up last night . . .'

'Wasn't it Eric Morcambe who said . . . ?'

'I think it was Bob Hope who remarked that . . .'

If you want to quote someone less well known, don't mention him or her by name. If you do, the reaction will probably be an audible 'Who?' Rather, say something like:

'Someone once said . . .'

or

'It has been said that . . .'

Alternatively, you could attribute the quote to someone more famous. Oddly enough, this ploy will immediately increase your audience's appreciation of those words of wit and wisdom. But make sure the person you name sounds as if he *could* have said that.

QUESTIONS AND ANSWERS

If a joke is funny, surely it's safe to tell to any audience?
Oh no it isn't! Some people may have found my vet and taxidermist gag offensive. A famous after dinner speaker toured the country, using pretty much the same speech. At one function he told his usual repertoire of jokes, including a story about a cat that got caught up a tree. The owner, an elderly lady, called the fire brigade, who arrived and rescued the cat. Out of gratitude the old lady insisted the firemen have a cup of tea and a slice of cake. When the firemen left, they reversed the fire engine off the drive – and ran over the cat!

The speaker was puzzled that not only did the story not get its usual laugh, but the rest of his speech was heard in complete silence. Only as he left did he discover he had muddled up his diary. He was not speaking, as he had thought, to the Conservative ladies of West Bromwich, but the West Bromwich branch of the RSPCA! Cat-lovers do not lap up tales about mangled moggies. Even the best gag in the world will bomb if the audience finds it offensive.

Is it ever worth risking risqué stories?
What is acceptable and what isn't in the content of a speech depends on so many factors that it would be foolish to attempt to lay down any hard and fast rules. However, it is worth pointing out that the law of diminishing returns applies to *all* subjects and styles and there are subjects other than one's bodily parts and functions.

How far should you go? The venue, the age and composition of the audience, even the time of day – all of these must be taken into consideration. Indelicate language at an afternoon charity affair in the village hall could easily create the speech from hell; a routine at a rugby club stag night would be disastrous if it were not as blue as the Danube.

SUMMARY

- All your material should be relevant to your theme and meaning- ful to your audience.

- Show them that you have a real comprehension of their specialised world.

- Devise, switch or borrow whatever material works for you.

- Don't feel bound by factual accuracy.

- Quotations should be spread thinly, like caviar, not piled on thickly like marmalade.

- Make them feel like a special group – which they are.

3

Targeting Humour and Compliments at Individuals

The contents of this chapter come with a health – and possibly wealth warning: *know your audience*. Sometimes even the friendliest little mockery of individuals present, even when made in the best possible taste, is totally unacceptable in an after dinner speech. But this is very rare: audiences generally expect to hear it – and victims usually love to receive it. Only you know the nature of the occasion and the attitude of any bigwigs likely to be present. If you don't, find out! If insults are out, fast forward to page 40.

Now that disclamer is out of the way, we can begin to have some fun. If your speech is to the members of a sports or social club, friendly jibes and a little banter are par for the course. In a corporate context you must be a little more wary. In this chapter we'll consider the relevance of irreverence. In particular, we'll discuss the importance of:

- Taking a few friendly pot shots.

- Sugaring your teasing remarks with praise.

- Dealing with hecklers and other distractions.

TAKING A FEW FRIENDLY POT SHOTS

At most dinners, a little friendly ribbing is called for. If properly done it shows the audience you've done your homework, it shifts attention away from you and onto them, and it bonds and re-inforces group spirit.

Choose your 'victims' with care; some people love being the centre of attention while others hate it. Ultimately it's a question of personality – both theirs and yours. To start your little grey cells working on this, here are three targets that are *usually* fair game and three others that should *usually* be treated as a protected species.

Three easy targets

Most audiences will feel perfectly comfortable if you target your humour at: yourself, local characters, your competitors or rivals.

Yourself

Mirror, mirror on the wall who's the fairest target of them all? Before you have a go at anyone else, you must first mock yourself. Let them see you're a good sport. Show them you don't take yourself too seriously:

> 'I'm such an unlucky guy . . . if I were reincarnated I'd probably come back as myself.'

> 'I'm smarter than I look. But then again I suppose I'd have to be.'

> 'They gave me a dope test . . . and I passed.'

Self-mockery of this kind is a subtle demonstration of your underlying self-confidence (honestly!). It offends nobody. More importantly though, it grants you licence to take a pop at others. If you are seen to be able to take it, it follows that you will be allowed to dish it out – and that's when the real fun starts.

Local characters

Every club, society and business has one or two larger-than-life characters. Bring them into your speech. But remember that your audience will only laugh at a parody of what it *recognises* as their little foibles. Ask yourself: *Why* are they considered to be characters? Is it something to do with the way they dress, their mannerisms, or perhaps their unusual jobs or strange hobbies?

The guests must recognise that while all your jokes are clearly exaggerations, they are nonetheless based on fundamental truths about your victims. For instance, there is no point in laughing at a character's colourful use of language, unless you are sure the audience knows he spends most of his waking hours effing and blinding, and is not merely the kind who just might bleat out an apologetic 'oh, blast' – and then only if mauled by a lion.

Say he is not known for his satorial elegance, then you might observe that:

> 'Doesn't (character) look wonderful? They made wonderful suits in the 1980s.'

If it's well known that he likes the odd gallon of booze:

> 'I've got some important news for you all: (character) just told me he's not going to drink anymore. Unfortunately, he's not going to drink any less either.'

If he's a high-flying legal eagle:

> 'I dreamt that (character) died and when he got to the gates of heaven he was interviewed by St Peter to see if he should be let into heaven or hell. "I don't know why I died so young," complained (character), "it doesn't seem fair, I'm only (age)." "I know," replied St Peter, "but according to all the time you've billed your clients for, you're at least 502." '

If his sole role in life seems to be to collect CDs:

> '(Character) has a magnificent CD collection. One day he went into a record shop and asked for 'Rhapsody in Blue', but the girl said they hadn't got it. "Well would you mind taking another look?" he asked. "Perhaps they do it in some other colour." '

Your competitors or rivals
A Prime Minister or President can unite his country and improve his personal approval rating at home by picking a fight with a weak opponent abroad. You can unite your organisation and improve your personal standing within it by having a go at corporate or sporting rivals who are not there to defend themselves. Let's suppose ABC Ltd and XYZ Ltd are fierce competitors. This is a story you could tell to ABC:

> 'A very rich man wanted to get his three sons started with businesses of their own, so he asked the oldest what he wanted. The boy said he wanted a phone company, so the man bought him British Telecom. The second son was a teenager. He said he liked burgers, so the man bought him McDonalds. The third son was younger and he loved cowboy outfits, so the man bought him XYZ.'

Obviously, the story works just as well if you're appearing before XYZ employees – provided you remember to change the punch line!

The high profile leader of a rival is also a legitimate target. Sir Richard Branson acquired the reputation of being an extremely keen, yet ultimately unsuccessful balloonist. When he came down to earth with a bang yet again, the following one-liner did the rounds: 'Well what do you expect when you put a prick in a balloon?' Today this joke would be ideal for an audience of BA workers, but it would go down like a lead balloon with people at Virgin Atlantic (well, they wouldn't laugh out loud anyway).

Three risky targets
Most people will enjoy being the butt of your jokes – but some won't. It is worth thinking twice – and then a third time – before targeting:

- your superiors

- your subordinates

- the audience generally.

Don't say anything in public to embarrass or undermine your bosses. They will not be amused and you may soon discover that UB40 is not just an old pop group. Similarly don't make jokes about junior staff. If you do, you'll come across as being a nasty, vindictive bully. If you have any doubts about *anyone's* likely reaction to a few well chosen jibes, *ask them* whether they would mind a little mickey taking.

And don't bite the hands that clap you. A group of plumbers won't consistently laugh at jokes based on the premise that plumbers are silly. Play it safe: give them what they want – jokes about their silly suppliers and customers.

SUGARING YOUR TEASING REMARKS WITH PRAISE

Never overlook the five elements of an after dinner speech which are almost impossible to overdo: the **welcome, congratulations, flattery, thanks** and **praise.**

A speech that is all humour – however good the humour – can sometimes become monotonous. You need some congratulatory and optimistic words to counterbalance your jokes and teasing roast lines. Your speech needs to be underpinned by some good, old-fashioned sincerity. So **welcome** your fellow guests, **congratulate** any previous speakers, **flatter** the top table, thank the catering staff . . . and **praise** . . . well praise just about everyone and everything.

If it moves, praise it; if it doesn't move, praise it. Praise the hosts ('nicest of people') the room ('these magnificent surroundings'), the occasion ('this wonderful event') and the meal ('it was nice to see the menu was in French . . . it made such a pleasant surprise each time the food arrived').

The problem is many of us are not very comfortable using gushing, extravagant language when praising individuals. Fortunately then, it's good to know that even effusive praise need not sound sycophantic in a speech. The same flattery that could appear too florid or subservient when spoken in private seems quite acceptable in a public tribute.

Combining a compliment and a tease

Funnily enough, a sincere compliment and a teasing jibe often fit well together, each reinforcing the other in a kind of verbal synergy. The trick is first to set up a situation which you can exploit with a teasing remark, before turning this into a genuine little compliment. If the praise comes immediately after the crowd has had a good laugh at your victim's expense, its effect will be at least doubled:

> 'When I asked (victim) about the wedding arrangements (**set-up**), he said, "Oh, I'll leave all that to you. But I do want Bells – and at least three cases of it" (**tease**). Well I don't know about Bells, but I work with (victim) at Grange Hill Comprehensive . . . and I can tell you that he is certainly one of the best Teachers I know (**praise**).'

Alternatively, you may wish to build up your victim before quickly bringing him down to earth with a bang. If so, you simply reverse your tease and praise, like this:

> '(Victim) is quite well off, you know (**set-up**). But he never brags about it (**praise**). In fact, you can sit in a pub with him all evening and never know he had a penny (**tease**).'

DEALING WITH HECKLERS AND DISTRACTIONS

You're most unlikely to be faced by loudmouth drunks or other nasty punters during an after dinner speech. It would be rather heavy-handed, if not churlish, for a speaker to learn professional anti-heckle lines for the purpose of silencing someone who is simply enjoying the evening. You want to show that you possess the superior wit, but to do so it shouldn't be necessary to grind your heckler into the ground.

Here are half-a-dozen fairly mild lines that you could use, if the situation *really* demands them:

'You know, you should be on TV – so we could turn you off.'

'Thank you. I used to know a funny version of that joke.'

'I look forward to running into you again – some day when you're walking and I'm driving.'

'Let's play pantomine horse. I'll be the front and you can be yourself.'

'I'm fascinated by what you have to say. I could sit and talk to you for minutes.'

'The next time you throw your old clothes away, why don't you stay in them?'

However, most interruptions during after dinner speeches are likely to be good-natured and restrained and they can often be really humorous and can add to the occasion. Don't have a go at anyone who makes a genuine attempt to get into the spirit of things. Thank them for their contribution:

'Can I book you for my next speech?'

One last word about answering hecklers: the wittiest sally in the world will count for naught if the heckle to which it gives rise is inaudible. An old trick of the politician is, therefore, to ask the heckler to repeat his remark. The room will then fall silent and the heckler may well fail to respond. In which case you could say: 'Lost for words? I'd like to help you out. Which way did you come in?' If he does repeat his remark it will now be heard loud and clear. More often than not the moment has passed, the timing has gone awry and the heckle will be greeted with total silence.

Latecomers, early leavers and other interrupters

At a formal dinner it would be quite improper to draw any attention to people coming and going during your speech.

However, at a more informal stag night type do, a few friendly put downs can work well.

To latecomers

'What time do you call this?'

'Nothing good on telly tonight?'

'Have you got a note? A fiver will do.'

To anyone leaving very soon after you've started to speak

'Hello, the critics are in.'

'There goes the only man with taste.'

'Had enough already? Chicken . . .'

To people returning

'I thought you'd be back after a wee while.'

'Don't be embarrassed – everyone's looking at you.'

'Could you hear us out there? . . . we could hear you in here.'

But don't take the rise out of anyone until you've established yourself as the likeable loveable chap that you are. I would also counsel restraint; once you have made remarks about someone turning up late or making a call of nature, it is best to get on with your speech and let any further disruptions go unnoticed.

QUESTIONS AND ANSWERS

Is it wise to mock a new kid on the block?
No, the audience will not grant you the right to make fun of a virtual stranger. Under these circumstances even words of mild mockery will sound highly insulting and your victim will wonder which planet you come from.

Is it acceptable to take verbal pot shots at women as well as at men?
That largely depends on *your* gender, sir. The times they are a-changin' and bawdy humour from women and about women today is now quite usual, in the right context. Girl power, and all that. Ginger, Scary, Posh and co had a lot to do with it. Women

are perfectly at liberty to spice up their speeches by saying pretty much what they want about men or women. This is not regarded as sexist. But men still need to be very wary about telling jokes against women – unless they 'started it' by heckling.

Does your victim always have to be known by the audience?
Yes, but the audience need not be known by your victim – or rather by your target, because not being there, he won't actually 'suffer'. Politicians are a classic example. A jibe at anyone currently active in the public arena takes on an extra cutting edge. Obviously your target will depend not on *your* political attitude but on the collective one of *your audience*:

'(Target) is the kind of guy Doctor Spooner would have referred to as a shining wit.'

'(Target) speaks his mind – which tends to limit his conversation a bit.'

'Men like him don't grow on trees – they swing from them.'

We often find politicians rather condescending, frightening, ridiculous or all three, and so perfect fodder for laughs.

SUMMARY

- Decide whether roasting is on the menu this evening. If it is, stick to the following guidelines.

- Show your audience that you don't take yourself too seriously.

- Don't roast anyone within your organisation unless it's appropriate, totally in character for the occasion, and clear to all that you don't really mean a word of it.

- Praise them too, even if it does hurt you to do so.

- Have a go at rivals too.

- Laugh along with anyone in the audience who makes a genuinely humorous contribution to the evening but put down any nasty hecklers swiftly, effectively, yet humanely.

4

Adding a Sparkle to Your Speech

Having something worthwhile to say is *never* enough. You need to know how to use words and images to reach your audience's minds and hearts. Your speech needs a touch of flair. Flair is partly intuition – which comes from experience, imagination, a willingness to think – and a careful study of this chapter!

If we face an important interview, we prepare ourselves to make the best possible impression. We *look* good. So, if we are about to meet an audience, we should polish our words as well as our shoes. We should *sound* good.

Today people's expectations are high and their attention spans are low. Merely to gain and hold an audience's attention requires flair. If your want to keep them interested, your speech must sparkle. So let's get polishing.

This chapter will explain how you can get your message across effectively by means of the following techniques:

- Using words to be said, not read.

- Choosing your words carefully.

- Engaging all the senses.

- Remembering rhythm.

USING WORDS TO BE SAID, NOT READ

Most people can write something to be *read*; few can write something to be *said*. Indeed, most people are unaware that there is even a difference.

We are used to writing things to be read. Such everyday written communication is known as **text**. What we are *not* used to doing is speaking our written words out loud. Writing intended to be spoken and heard is known as **script.**

Every effective after dinner speaker *must* recognise that there are very important differences between text and script, namely:

Text	Script
• is a journey at the reader's pace	• is a journey at the speaker's pace
• can be re-read, if necessary	• is heard once, and only once
• can be read in any order.	• is heard in the order it is spoken.

Therefore, you must prepare a speech for an audience which cannot listen at its own pace; which cannot ask you to repeat parts it did not hear or understand; and which cannot choose the order in which to consider your words.

Spoken words are structured in time; written words are structured in space. Communicating in a purely spoken form demands that the listener always keeps up with the speaker. Simultaneous comprehension is essential. Breaking up a thought into separate elements, into a sequence of short, simple, one-thought sentences or part-sentences, is one way of ensuring this.

A degree of repetition is needed. Important ideas, facts and opinions must be continually reinforced to ensure the listener is kept in the picture. And a word, phrase or sentence may need to be repeated if it was drowned by laughter the first time round.

The order of words is different, too. We seem subconsciously to understand the best words and phrases and the best order of words and phrases when we *speak* but to lose the knack when we *write* script.

The lesson is clear: **Speak your words out loud before you commit them to paper**. You will find that each element, each phrase, each sentence, will be built from what has gone before. Instinctively, you will take your listeners from:

• the known to the unknown

• the general to the particular

• the present to the future.

CHOOSING YOUR WORDS CAREFULLY

There is no specific and correct way to express thoughts. You have a choice of words, many with subtle variations of meaning and tone. You have a choice of word patterns that can create vivid pictures, touch the emotions and stay in people's minds. Think of choosing *effective* language rather than *correct* language.

Painting word pictures

Watching a story unfold before your eyes is dramatic and memorable. The characters move. The scenes are in colour. The whole thing has life. Merely listening to a wordy description, however enthusiastically delivered, is a yawn.

Today most people are used to *watching* TV, not *listening* to radio. You need to give your jokes and stories a visual aspect. The way to do this is to paint word pictures that allow an audience's own imagination to take over. Let them 'see' the scenes you are describing. This means avoiding vague references to *food* and replacing them with *pizzas* and *kebabs*. Use adjectives that conjure up specific images and trigger the senses: a *spicy* curry, a *fruity* jelly, a *savoury* pudding.

> 'Let me tell you something about (local character). Soon after we met, he invited me to his 30th (or whatever) birthday party and he gave me details of his address and how to get there. He said, "a number 8 bus will bring you right to my door – 69 Della Street. Walk up to the front door and press the doorbell with your elbow." "Why my elbow?" I asked. "Because you'll have the wine in one hand and my prezzie in the other, won't you?" '

Give the audience the right detail and they can *see* your word picture. And one picture is worth a thousand words.

Using warm words

Words are powerful. They conjure images, evoke emotions and trigger responses deep within us so we react, often without knowing why. So-called *warm* words make us feel secure and comfortable, while *cold* words leave us uneasy and unsure. Writer Henry James said the two most beautiful words in the English language are *summer afternoon*, because they evoke just the right emotions.

In the early days of instant coffee, advertisers got off to a bad start by stressing words like *quick*, *time-saving* and *efficient*. These are all words without warmth and feeling. Makers of fresh coffee fought back with warm, happy, appetising words like *aroma*, *fresh* and *tasty*. Makers of instant coffee soon learned the lesson and their product became *delicious*, *rich* and *satisfying*. Sales *blossomed*. The rest, as they say, is history.

Once you get into the habit of looking at the emotional colouring of words, as well as their meanings, you will find yourself using the kind of language that puts listeners at ease and encourages them to react more favourably to your speeches and to you.

Selecting similes

A simile is like a love song. It proves nothing yet describes so much. It makes abstract ideas imaginable. Reach for vivid comparisons. Help your listeners understand and remember. Invent tomorrow's clichés.

'As delicate as a whisper.'

'As inflexible as an epitaph.'

'As cold as outer space.'

Don't say, 'her anger showed in her eyes', but rather, 'her eyes were flaming like chip pans'.

Making use of metaphors

A metaphor is a pair of spectacles we wear in order that things can be seen more clearly. It extends our language as we transfer our thought processes from one set of words to another. Unlike a simile, it provides a single image, which must be viewed through bifocals:

'The sullen sky leaned against the rooftop.'

'Trees marinated the morning mist.'

'Thoughts wriggled in my head.'

Using imagery

Imagery is the implanting of word pictures in listeners' minds to illustrate, illuminate and embellish a speaker's thoughts. Which of the two following rhetorical questions has the greater impact on you?

'Can we continue to allow so many hundreds of pedestrians to be killed on our roads each year?'

'How would you feel if the doorbell rang, you opened the door, and there, at your feet, lay the dead body of your child?'

No contest. The first question may make you *think*. The second will make you *feel*. If you *tell* them they may *listen*; if you *show* them they will *pay attention*; if you *involve* them they will *react*. The purpose of imagery is not to decorate, but to assist the purpose of the speaker.

Images can move the argument forward more cogently than pure reason. The reaction you seek is both surprise and familiarity. A paradox? Yes. It is not the shocking surprise that makes you scream 'Eureka!' in your bath. It is the satisfying surprise you feel at the denouement of an Agatha Christie play – a surprise that makes you smile and gently nod your head in acknowledgement of a job well done.

ENGAGING ALL THE SENSES

Sensory details bring breadth and depth to your descriptions Why? Because you want your audience to believe in your anecdotes, to feel they have left their seats for a few moments and are 'living' within the story. This can happen only if the world you describe has all the trappings of the real world. And the real world is a sensory experience.

Take the sense of smell. How can you use it to help describe a dislikeable character? Give him breath that smells of *drains*. A pleasant girl? Try *lemon-scented* hair. An elderly well-to-do bridge-playing couple? The odours of *cigars*, *mothballs* and *Earl Grey tea*. Pepper your descriptions with sensory detail. It will bring your anecdotes to life like a shot of whisky in a cup of coffee.

We can learn a lot from writers of popular fiction. Take a look at this extract from *The Fallen Curtain* by Ruth Rendell:

'Tea was lovely at gran's. Fish and chips that she didn't fetch from the shop but cooked herself, cream meringues and chocolate eclairs, tinned peaches with evaporated milk, the lot washed down with fizzy lemonade.'

How much more effective this is than simply saying 'Gran doted on me and spoilt me something rotten at tea-time.'

Here Stephen King uses sensory details to bring a character to life in *Carrie*:

> 'Norma led them around the dance floor to their table. She exuded odours of Avon soap, Woolworth's perfume and Juicy Fruit gum.'

And how about this from Katherine Mansfield:

> 'Alexander and his friend in a train. Spring . . . wet lilac . . . sprouting rain.'

So few words yet the wetness is palpable.

REMEMBERING RHYTHM

A good speech should attract and hold an audience as a magnet attracts and holds iron filings. Here are four simple techniques that will add an almost magical, melodic quality to your speeches:

- the rule of three
- parallel sentences
- alliteration
- repetition.

Let's take each in turn.

The rule of three

Lyricists know they must always include a simple yet memorable 'hook' in their songs (the part you can't stop humming). One of the most effective is a three-word, three-phase, or three-sentence hook: 'She loves you, yeah, yeah, yeah'. The best speechwriters use the same technique. People like to hear speakers talk to the beat of three:

> 'Things have changed a lot over the last 50 years: from the Home Guard to home computers, from Vera Lynn to Vera Duckworth, from ration cards to scratchcards.'

Three is a magic number for speechmakers. It doesn't sound quite
so effective in twos and fours, but fives and sevens work almost as
well.

Parallel sentences
Sentences that are parallel add a rhythmic beauty that helps an
audience anticipate and follow equal ideas:

> 'To change is normal. Nothing is constant except change. Our
> interest rates change . . . Our clothes change . . . Our cars
> change . . . The face of our workforce changes . . . Our politics
> change . . . Our philosophies change . . . Even our cultures
> change. Change has become the status quo. Change is the only
> thing that's the same. That's normal.'

Alliteration

> 'Looking and loving our behaviours pass
> The stones, the steels and the polished glass.'

The repetition of sounds and syllables, usually at the beginning
of words, can help create a mood or unite a section of script.
Alliteration can make your speeches special and spellbinding:

> 'A generation ago we feared typhoid more than terrorists
> . . . cholera more than crack . . . and rickets more than re-
> dundancy.'

Repetition
If there is anything that is almost guaranteed to make an audience
break out into spontaneous applause it is a repetition of strong,
emotive words:

> 'We will fight, and fight, and fight again to save the Party we
> love.'

However, use the wrong words and it will fall flat. How does
this sound?

> 'We will tussle, and tussle, and tussle again to protect the Party
> we are fond of.'

'She likes you, yes, yes, yes.'

It doesn't work, does it?

QUESTIONS AND ANSWERS

How can I learn to create powerful and effective metaphors?
Try experimenting with nouns and verbs. Get a sheet of paper.
Write a list of nouns down the left side and a list of verbs down
the right. Anything will do – tables, computers, storms, soap,
saxophones; falling, boiling, dressing, dancing, drinking. Now mix
and match the verbs with the nouns, looking for combinations that
strike you as piquant, and put them into sentences.

The trick is to focus on secondary characteristics. When we
think of *boiling*, for example, the first thing that comes to mind is
heat and *steam*. What else does boiling do? It melts things, turning
them into liquid. So if we combine boil with storm, for example
we might come up with: *The storm boiled the ground into instant
mud pudding.* Result: an instant and powerful image of a quag-
mire. With a little practice you will find a new world of linguistic
possibilities opening up for you.

*What is the best way to build up a personal thesaurus of original
similes?*
Make a list of common descriptive similes and then rewrite each
with one or two alternative comparisons. For example, *quiet as a
lamb* could become *quiet as a locked door* or *quiet as a Celtic
supporter at the Rangers end*. Start with these: slow as a tortoise;
clean as a whistle; sick as a parrot.

Once you get used to rewriting similes, start creating your own
from scratch: *icebergs* . . . as tall as cathedrals; *suave* . . . as a row
of head waiters; *inconspicuous* . . . as the Invisible Man. Now, over
to you: *music* . . . ; *profitable* . . . ; *dynamic* . . .

*Are there any other special linguistic devises I can use to add a
sparkle to my speeches?*
Here are some more figures of speech to experiment with to see if
they can be used or adapted to suit your style:

- **Hyperbole.** Exaggeration for effect: *I've told you millions of
times not to exaggerate.*

- **Irony.** The meaning is conveyed by words whose literal meaning is the opposite: *Don't worry. It doesn't matter if we lose the order and our jobs.*

- **Antithesis.** Contrasting thoughts are placed side by side for emphasis: *Some rise by sin and some fall by virtue.*

- **Paradox.** A statement which on first hearing seems absurd or contradictory, but isn't: *I'm sorry this speech is so long: I didn't have enough time to make it shorter.*

- **Oxymoron.** Two contradictory terms are combined to form a phrase: *It was a bitter sweet experience.*

- **Zeugma.** A verb is applied to two nouns, though strictly appropriate to only one of them: *We sang their songs and their praise.*

- **Personification.** Inanimate or abstract objects are treated as though they were human: *The factory breathes new life.*

But don't overdo it. A budding orator once sent an outline of his latest speech to the finest speechmaker in the land for his advice. The manuscript was returned with the words, 'SPEECH FINE, JUST NEEDS SOME POLISH', scribbled at the bottom. When he eventually rose to his feet, his audience was startled to hear a speech on cake-making containing numerous quotations from Stanislas Przybyszewski and Eliza Orzeszkowa. The lesson to be learned is that unless you are certain that your final touches really assist and enhance your speech, leave them out. Technique must not get in the way of the message.

SUMMARY

- Think like a listener and write like a talker. Say your words out loud before you commit them to paper. Use *effective* language, not necessarily *correct* language.

- Use words and images creatively and imaginatively and your speech will come to life. Things happen in the minds and hearts of your audience. If you look into their eyes, you can see it happen. It's a great experience.

- The world is a sensory experience. Your speech should be, too. Allow your audience to do far more than just *listen* to your speech. Let them *see* it, *taste* it, *smell* it, *touch* it. Let them *experience* it.

- It is important that what you say *sounds* good. Your speech should have its own rhythm. Give it light and shade, valleys and peaks. A landscape of valleys and peaks will keep an audience interested and involved. People need valleys before they can see peaks.

5

Preparing Your Script

It's time to lay out the shape of your speech and look at the basic elements in its construction. 'Where shall I begin?' the White Rabbit asked the King. 'Begin at the beginning, and go on till you come to the end: then stop', came the reply. Wrong, Your Majesty! Start with the middle, and go on to the beginning and the end: and then stop it. Draft the main body of your speech first – *then* top-and-tail it.

In this chapter we shall consider the importance of:

- Structuring your speech.

- Hooking your audience.

- Ending on the right note.

- Bracketing your speech.

STRUCTURING YOUR SPEECH

By now, you may have collected, devised or switched a score or more of stories, friendly insults and other one-liners which are, of course, all highly entertaining and in keeping with the tone and theme of your address. However, your collection is not yet a speech. It's like building a house, and you've only just had the bricks delivered.

Now you have to arrange your material in a logical order so it will glide smoothly, like a narrative. This is known as **structuring**, or **routining**. There's little more tedious for an audience than having to sit through a collection of disconnected jokes and stories. In a well structured speech everything flows effortlessly to a natural conclusion – to a high point – as each joke and anecdote draws them in and pulls them along.

Good structuring also improves your lines, allows you to be more concise, and creates a kind of comedy synergy. Each joke is not only complete unto itself; it develops naturally from a previous thought and serves as a set-up for the material that follows. The entertainment value of the entire speech becomes greater than the sum of the entertainment value of its component parts.

A well structured speech will:

- attract attention

- hold interest

- be memorable.

Varying the texture

An audience will be shell-shocked by a constant barrage of quick-fire one-liners, but equally it will be put to sleep by a whole series of long and slow anecdotes. If you are going to keep your audience entertained you need to continually vary your style and pace. And you need to be a little unpredictable.

A basic framework

Many speakers find it best to begin a talk with a cleverly constructed series of strong humorous one-liners. Later you may wish to relate an *occasional* longer story to lend variety, and to provide your audience with a breather from all those hysterically funny one-liners and brief quips with which you began, and which you will intersperse between – and even include within – the lengthier stories.

This start-fast end-slow approach is a useful basic framework for any after dinner speech, but it can and should be adjusted as necessary to suit the requirements of specific audiences. The nature and composition of your fellow diners should not only influence *what* you say, but also, to a large extent, *how* you say it.

Being flexible

Think audience. A useful trick is to think of the kinds of programmes they probably watch on television. Are they more likely to be devotees of *Never Mind the Buzzcocks* or *Parkinson*? If you bear in mind the probable tastes of your audience as you structure your speech, you are far more likely to construct a script that they will find entertaining. Certainly, you need to vary the texture throughout, but you need to *bias* it either towards a stand-up or laid back approach, towards snappy one-liners (*Buzzcocks*) or longer humorous anecdotes (*Parky*).

The good news is that as you begin to construct and rehearse your speech, you will find a natural rhythm will develop automatically. By imagining that a typical member of your audience is sitting opposite you, without even consciously thinking about it you will instinctively know when it's time to speed up or slow down – when it's time to include a few complimentary remarks, a cheeky little insult, a more thought provoking interlude.

Keeping them in the picture
Your family car has stopped at a picnic spot. There is a map of the area and an arrow pointing to your location with the words: 'You are here.' Little Johnny reads it and turns to you with a puzzled expression. 'How do they know?' he asks. The answer for your listeners is because you have provided them with a simple route map. Within the first few minutes of your speech you have told them where you will be taking them, and possibly how long the journey will take:

'I once climbed a mountain and asked a man in a cave, "What's the secret of financial success?" And he said, "If I knew that, do you really think I'd be buggering around up here in this bloody cave?" Well I think I've now come up with a few answers myself. During the next half-hour I'm going to suggest three ways we can all improve our financial success . . . If you happen to come across that fool on the hill, perhaps you could tip him the wink . . .'

An enjoyable journey has begun with all your amusing stories and reminiscences forming the backdrop to this theme.

The highs and lows of humour
Structuring enhances a speech by taking advantage of the natural peaks and valleys of humour. Each line in a speech cannot have the same degree of funniness: if each did, the monologue would become monotonous. The softer jokes can make the strong jokes even stronger, and some of the strong jokes can be used to help the softer ones along. Just as a varied rhythm and intensity in a piece of music adds anticipation and excitement, so your comedy peaks and valleys should be staggered. Naturally, you want more peaks than valleys, but so long as you have to have the valleys you might as well take advantage of them.

The showbiz adage of doing your best stuff *first* still applies.

Once you have won your audience over they will even find less strong material hilarious; but of course you will keep a sure-fire barn-stormer for the finish.

There are no hard and fast rules to assembling a script. It often comes down to a gut feeling. Humour is so subjective that in a group of half a dozen jokes, few people will agree which is the biggie you should build up to. However, the mechanics of structuring are fairly simple.

Getting it together

Many people find it easiest to structure their speeches using a word processor. If you prefer not to fight with your computer, you can cut and paste manually. Use a separate card for each joke and story and then lay each subtopic out from first to last gag. This makes the material physically easier to arrange because everything is unattached. You can play around with your cards until that Condor moment when you hit just the order that satisfies you. Then staple or glue them together in readiness for some minor re-writing.

Re-writing

After you've arranged your material in logical progression and read it through again, you'll find the individual jokes and stories just don't fit together properly. Each was written as a separate entity; now they need to be re-written to create at least the illusion of a flowing narrative.

Weaving in and out of jokes

A joke needs a set-up, a context. It should not be told in isolation. It should arise naturally from whatever preceded it and its punch-line should allow you to embark smoothly on your next topic. Try to choose jokes and stories that have a telling point. In that way, if the tale fails to win a laugh, you can go on talking as if you never meant it to.

This example comes from a talk given to an audience of young mums. Notice how the speaker follows the simple format of: **Into story, Story, Out of story**. The anecdote is set up, told, and its punch line allows her to move on, in this case to make a more serious point:

Into story: Sometimes the walls seem to close in on you. You have to get out of the house.

Story: Last week I was walking in the park with my five children when a friendly gardener asked, 'Are all those children yours, or is it a picnic?' 'They're all mine,' I replied 'and it's certainly no picnic!'

Out of story: And we all know how difficult life can be at times, don't we . . . ?

Smoothing out the rough edges

You may have too many similar gags close to each other. The wording of some jokes may be too repetitive. A story may no longer need to be set up because a previous line now provides the necessary context. All these problems and others can be taken care of with some minor adjustments.

For example, suppose you have written these three jokes about your family's proud military tradition:

'My great-great grandfather fell at Waterloo . . . someone pushed him off platform nine.'

'My grandpa had a very proud service career, in the Army. He fought with Mountbatten in Burma, with Alexander in Tunis, with Monty at Alamein . . . he couldn't get on with anyone.'

'My grandpa wore Her Majesty's uniform at the Crimea. Victoria was not amused though. Said it fitted her much better.'

Obviously the set-ups are too similar for jokes so close together and the routine doesn't flow. One solution would be to change the order, change your 'great-great grandfather' into 'an ancestor' and claim you wore Her Majesty's uniform. Here's a possible re-write:

'My grandpa had a very proud service career, in the Army. Oh yes – he fought with Mountbatten in Burma, with Alexander in Tunis, with Monty in Alamein . . . he couldn't get on with anyone . . . but I've been in the Army myself, you know. Did my National Service. For two years I wore Her Majesty's uniform . . . 'course it fitted her better . . . but I come from an old military family . . . one of my ancestors fell at Waterloo . . . some bugger pushed him off platform nine.'

There should be three good laughs here, each progressively louder and more sustained.

Keeping it flowing

Have you noticed how entertainers, politicians and TV presenters move easily and unobtrusively from one topic to another? Like them, you can make your speech flow smoothly and gracefully from beginning to end by making use of link words and bridges. You use these techniques in everyday conversation without ever thinking about them. Link words are simply words or phrases used to keep things flowing as you discuss one particular topic. Bridges are words or phrases that allow you to change topics without ever sounding abrupt. In the following excerpt from an after dinner speech to young farmers, the link words are in italics and the bridges are in bold print. We begin with some soft one-liners about holidays and honeymoons – which would work with most audiences – before bridging to a few animal crackers – which were particularly suited to *this* audience:

> '*Did I tell you* we went on holiday in April? . . . I like to get in early while the sheets are still clean. We went to (local resort). It was a sort of sentimental journey . . . the wife and me spent our honeymoon there. We had a nice wedding – just a quiet family affair . . . just me, the wife and the kids . . . her mother couldn't make it – she was on manoeuvres at the time.'

> '*But I remember* that first night so well. There we were, tucked up in bed with the moonlight streaming through the holes in the ceiling . . . the wife snuggled up to me and said, "Mr (your surname) . . . well, we hadn't known each other very long . . . Mr (your surname), will you love me in the hereafter?" I said, "If I don't get what I'm here after, you'll be here after I've gone!" '

> '*So anyway*, we decided to go back there again this year. **Had a nasty accident on the way, though.** I was driving down this country lane when a big rooster flapped out through a gap in the hedge – straight under my front wheels! Killed it stone dead. Terrible! The farmer saw what happened and as I got out of the car he came running over to me and started carrying on something alarming. "Oh, my prize rooster! My prize rooster!" I said, "I'm very sorry, mate, but it really wasn't my fault. I'll replace him if you like." He said, "All right – the hen-coop's just behind the barn." '

'He was a funny chap though, that farmer. I noticed that he'd neatly ploughed most of his big field but he'd left one corner untouched. It was a right mess. So I asked him why. He said, "You're quite right, son, I never could touch that spot. That bit of the field has sacred memories for me – it were right there, on that very spot, that I were first introduced to the delights of loving. Right there. I can remember it like it were yesterday – and you see that gap in the hedge just there? Well, her mother used to stand right there, chewing away and a-watching us!" I says, "She used to stand there, chewing away and a-watching you! Didn't she say anything?" "Oh ar," he says, "baaaaa!" . . . wicked old devil, having me on like that . . . least I *think* he was having me on.'

'I had to go though. Couldn't hang around any longer. Had to be in (same local resort) by eight or we'd miss the meal. By now the farmer's milking a cow outside the barn. I asked him the time 'cos my watch wasn't working – must have been broken in that smash with the rooster. So he lifts up the (mime lifting up udders) . . . that's right . . . and he says, "It's just turned ten past seven." I was right baffled so I went back to the car and fetched the wife. "Would you mind telling me again what the time is," I said, 'cos I wanted the missus to see, like. So again the old boy lifts up the (mime) . . . that's right . . . and he says, "It's coming up to quarter past seven." So I says, "That's amazing. How do you tell the time by lifting up the er . . . er?" "Well," he says, "if I do that . . . (mime lifting with right hand) . . . It's no good, and if I do that (mime lifting with left hand) . . . it's no good, and if I do that (mime lifting with both hands peering underneath) . . . I can just see the clock tower down the village . . . !" '

'As we were leaving, I asked the wife . . . (and on we move, to pastures new . . .)'

Editing

A speech is like a pair of shoes: it will always benefit from a little more polishing. There is no speech that cannot be improved by cutting, chopping, eliminating. Prune away the dead wood, the redundant, the rhetorical flourishes, anything that doesn't sound like you. Make it tight, direct, to the point and – most importantly of all – make it entertaining. After your first edit put your draft away and don't look at it for a few days. When you go back to it you will see much more clearly what needs to be tightened, improved, weeded out.

Getting it down on paper

The best talkers are those who are most natural. They are easy, fluent, friendly and amusing. No script for them. How could there be? They are talking only to us and basing what they say on our reactions as they go along. For most of us, however, that sort of performance is an aspiration rather than a description. Our tongues are not so honeyed and our words are less winged. We need a script.

There is always a best order *for you* to make your points and tell your gags, there is a best way of conveying yourself. There are best words and phrases. Quite soon you discover that any genuinely spontaneous performance is not practicable so it might as well be scripted. The trick is to let your speech have the *appearance* of a friendly chat between intimate pals so that the humour arises out of your persona with apparent spontaneity.

But what sort of script? Cards? Notes? Speech written out in full? It's up to you. Here are a few personal preferences:

- Word processed notes, headlines or full script on A4 paper.

- 16 or 18 point, Century Gothic or Times New Roman type styles, single or double spaced.

- One side and top half of the paper only; bottom half blank. This keeps your notes well up any lectern you may be using and your head up to face the audience.

Think carefully about what suits you best and evolve a personal style. Its very familiarity will, in time, become part of its usefulness. Whatever form your script takes, look at it openly. Having a script means you're prepared. Don't be ashamed of it.

HOOKING YOUR AUDIENCE

You must grab your audience's attention from the word go. However, you cannot sensibly decide which hook to employ until *after* you have structured the middle section of your speech. Only then can you select an opening that is appropriate, in keeping with the tone and content of the rest of the speech, and interesting to your audience.

A tourist once stopped his car in an Irish village and asked the way to Dublin. 'If I were you,' replied the thoughtful local, 'I wouldn't start from here.' You at least have the luxury of choosing where to begin your journey:

> 'Ladies and Gentlemen, tonight I am going to suggest three reasons why this company should be interested in closer relations with Europe . . . Ingrid Bergman, Bridget Bardot and David Ginola . . . The perfect argument for embracing our continental cousins, for greater and varied intercourse with our fellow Europeans . . .'

You have simultaneously introduced your theme – the need to develop stronger ties with Europe – loosened collars and set the mood. You have told them: 'Don't worry folks, there may be an important message here, but this speech is going to be fun!'

Your opening *must* be interesting. Here are three of the best devices that can be used to hook an after dinner audience:

- The **question hook**.

- The **anniversary hook**.

- The **humour hook**.

The manner of your approach will depend on your personal style, your audience and the image you wish to project.

The question hook
This is a common enough oratorical device, but one all too often neglected by after dinner speakers. The hook can take many forms. Here are three dependables:

Tonight's the night
What is different and special about tonight? What will the audience get out of it? You need to be topical, personal and relevant:

> 'What is it about this evening that makes it different from any other? Would you like to know the *real* reason why (some

serious event) happened? Then buckle your seat belt. It ain't
what you think . . .'

The *real* reason. Funny or serious, this is going to be interesting.
You have their undivided attention.

Getting them thinking
Here you open with a question that makes everyone present ask it
of themselves. They are forced to make a small private assessment
of themselves:

> 'What would you do if you won the Lottery . . . Save, share or
> splurge?'

Such a question immediately involves the audience and makes
them readier to pay attention to what follows.

Being off the wall
Your question appears to have no relevance whatsoever, and
perhaps it hasn't:

> 'Where do flies go in the winter?'

Or maybe you'll tell them at the end.

The anniversary hook
There's nothing like telling people what a special day it is today.
You're telling them that 'today's the day!'

> 'Ladies and Gentlemen, this is a truly historic day! This day, the
> 18th of June, will always be remembered because of three
> world-shattering events. Napoleon finally met his Waterloo
> at Waterloo in 1815, pop superstar Sir Paul McCartney had
> his first day on earth in 1942, and on this day in 200X, you
> attended tonight's banquet and heard the finest damned after
> dinner speech of your entire lifetime! Now . . . who's going to
> make it?'

You can find plenty of birthdays and anniversaries listed in
specialist books (*Making a Wedding Speech*, in this series, for
example, has no less than 732 of them). You'll also find them in
most daily and Sunday newspapers.

The humour hook

A humorous opening must be fresh, to the point, told as succinctly as possible and timed so that the punch line will elicit a laugh. A self-deprecating opening almost always works – it puts the audience with you, not against you. Here are some examples. They are all tried and tested so you don't need to worry about choosing a dud:

'As soon as I stand up some fool always begins to talk.'

'As Henry VIII said to each of his wives in turn: "I shall not keep you long." '

'Ladies and Gentlemen – the ladies is over there (pointing), and the gents is over there' (pointing).

'Good Ladies, evening and Gentlemen . . . I *knew* I should have rehearsed this speech.'

'I got out of my sickbed to be here . . . my girlfriend's got 'flu.'

'Ladies and Gentlemen, I won't take long. This suit has to be back in 20 minutes.'

'What do you think of the dinner jacket? I'm breaking it in for a waiter.'

'I've been asked to say a few words because . . . well, the staff want to get home in time for *Friends*, and they figured that if I made a speech it would be the quickest way to clear the room.'

'I've just revised my speech to make a short reference to (possibly some aspect of the meal). Churchill was always re-writing his speeches until he had to give them. But that's where my similarity to Churchill ends.'

'It's hard to be funny when you have to be clean.'

'I must admit that I've made a very similar speech to this before. Once to the patients at Broadmoor, once to the Flat Earth Society, South-East Branch, and once to the Penzance Haemorrhoid Sufferer's Society – a stand-up buffet. So to those of you who have heard this speech three times already, I apologise.'

'May I begin by thanking you for the three great human qualities – faith, hope and charity. Your applause before I speak, that's faith. Applause during my speech, that's hope. Applause after my speech, that's charity.'

'I should have been at my mother-in-law's funeral in Scotland today, but business before pleasure.'

'The last time I made an after dinner speech someone at the rear shouted, "I can't hear you!" – and a man sitting next to me yelled back, "I'll change places with you!" '

'The last time I made an after dinner speech here a man fell asleep. You could have heard his snoring in (local) Street. So I asked the waiter to wake him and do you know what the cheeky so-and-so replied? He said, "You wake him. You were the one who put him to sleep." '

'This is the first time I have spoken after dinner, except during other people's speeches.'

'Thank you, I appreciate your welcome because I just felt slightly unwell. I told our sympathetic chairman that I was feeling funny and he said, "Well, do your speech before it wears off." '

'Your chairman just asked me, "Would you like to speak now, or should we let our guests enjoy themselves a little longer?" '

'We've got a mixed bag for you this evening. She should be here at about ten.'

(When asked to make a 20 minute speech.) 'I've been asked to speak for 40 minutes . . . (Pretend that someone is whispering something to you.) Oh sorry, apparently I've been asked to speak for just 20 minutes.' (Rip your notes in half and throw one pile away.)

'I've got some good news and some bad news. First, the bad news – after writing and re-writing, editing and re-editing, the very shortest I could make this speech for is one hour 14 minutes. That was the bad news . . . now for the good news – I was lying about the bad news.'

'Ladies and Gentlemen, first the good news: when I first saw (local character's) new suit this evening. I was absolutely speechless . . . Now the bad news: I've almost recovered from the shock, and the speech must go on.'

'Ladies and Gentlemen, my dad taught me always to remember the ABC and the XYZ of speechmaking. ABC: always be concise. XYZ examine your zip' (look down).

'Thank you for that introduction and applause. You're just like my first wife – you build me up for one minute, then make me do all the work for the next half-hour.'

'Tonight I'm appearing free of charge, and I think you'll agree I'm worth every penny of it.'

'I feel like the young Arab Sheikh who inherited his father's harem. I know exactly what to do, but where on earth do I begin?'

'For those of you at the back, if you can't see me properly, I look very much like Brad Pitt/Kate Winslett. For those of you at the front . . . please don't tell the ones at the back.'

'Ladies and Gentlemen – well your chairman did ask me to begin with a gag.'

'Thank you. I'm not crazy about making speeches, but I've been married for 25 years and this is the only chance I get to see if my voice still works.'

'Ladies and Gentlemen – who says flattery doesn't pay.'

'I've been asked not to bore you with a long speech this evening . . . so I'm going to do my best to bore you with a short one.'

'I've been to some really tremendous black-tie events in the last few months, but looking around here, I can safely say that this is by far the most . . . recent.'

'My Lords, Ladies, Gentlemen, Dukes, Royal Princes, Foreign Ambassadors . . . I know none of you are in tonight, but that shows you the kind of audience I'm used to playing to.'

(After a formal introduction by a toastmaster.) 'Ladies and Gentlemen, did he say pray *for* the silence of John Smith?'

Your opening sentence is the *second* most important of your speech. Yes, you've guessed it: the most important sentence is your *last*.'

ENDING ON THE RIGHT NOTE

A **closer** is to a speech what a high note is to an aria. It is the candescence that should trigger applause. And a shrewdly chosen line which combines truth with fun is a far more popular finale than a glum old proverb or a plea for people to attend next month's fete. As you drive over that final hill, you say: 'Look, everyone, there's the sea!'

'And that, Mesdames and Messieurs, is my pièce de résistance, otherwise known as my little French virgin. Bon soir et merci bien.'

If you can find the ideal ending you will inject that ultimate bit of magic into your one-person-show. Your closing words should provide a delectable and memorable dessert with a delicious aftertaste. Bob Monkhouse found the perfect finish to an after dinner speech where the guest of honour was a millionaire, well known for his left-wing politics and outspoken honesty about himself:

'Len uncorked a Jeroboam of Don Perignon, and poured me a mugful. "Len," I said, "what is your political philosophy; what do you consider the purpose of government?" Unhesitatingly, and very earnestly, he replied, "The greatest good for the greatest number." "And what," I asked, "do you consider to be the greatest number?" And Len said, "Number One" . . . Ladies and Gentlemen, the toast is . . . Number One!" '

Follow that! Yet a very similar story was told about the scholar and philosopher David Hume 200 years earlier. Mr Monkhouse had concluded that the length of time since it was last aired in public, and the odds against there being a student of 18th century literature in the room were both long enough to justify the story's inclusion.

If you can find an apposite line by Dr Johnson, Voltaire or Genghis Khan that would perfectly round off your talk, make any necessary little adjustments here and there and say it with confidence. Use whatever material answers your needs. Your speech will not be reviewed by literary critics. But always remember the Eleventh Commandment: Thou shalt not be found out!

On 6th September 1901 President McKinley was assassinated.

Some people might know the year, but who would know the precise date, other possibly than Mrs McKinley? And she's unlikely to be in the audience. So why not claim that *today* is the anniversary. I won't tell.

'In conclusion, Ladies and Gentlemen, this day marks another significant anniversary. On this day, (today's date), back in 1901, US President William McKinley was making a speech when some fellow shot him dead. Now I'm not much of one for believing in signs and omens, but there's no point in tempting fate, so I think I'll sit down.'

Here are some other classic comedy closers that you could use, adopt or personalise:

'As I said to the woman I lost my virginity to, thanks for laughing.'

'If you didn't find it funny tonight it's art and you'll find it hilarious when I'm dead.'

'I must go now – if I'm not back by 11 the wife lets out my room.'

'I must go now – if I'm not in bed by 11 I always go home.'

'I must go now – I've got another booking – next July.'

'I must go now – my mother-in-law's out on parole.'

'I must go now – I've got a fair bit to do back at the office.'

'I must go now – I've got to get back to John O'Groats – and John's a very demanding lad.'

'And please drive home safely. We'd all much rather talk *to* you than *about* you.'

'And please – don't learn the Highway Code by accident. Try to drive so that your licence expires before you do.'

'Before I left home this evening, my little girl said to me: "Daddy, I hope they clap you and clap you and clap you after you speak. If they don't I'll cry and cry forever and ever." Ladies and Gentlemen, I leave it to you – do you want to be responsible for a child being miserable for the rest of her life?'

'Remember, there are Seven Deadly Sins, enough for one each day . . . have a nice week!'

'A final thought. Always keep your words nice and sweet . . . because you never know when you're going to have to eat them.'

'Before I sit down I'd like to thank you for being a wonderful audience . . . and you can feel proud because I'm very hard to please.'

'Finally, I'd like to thank (organiser) without whose help this would all have been – so much easier.'

'Don't clap too hard – it's a very old building.'

'Ladies and Gentlemen, I've been Pat Smith and you've been great.'

'Do be careful as you go home. Did you know that one man is knocked down in (county) every five minutes? And he's getting pretty fed up with it.'

You have reached your destination in style and now for the applause.

BRACKETING YOUR SPEECH

This is a device usually associated with seasoned pros. It is designed not only to grab an audience's attention at the *start* of a speech, but also – and at the same time – to set up a situation that can be exploited at the *end*. The idea is to present your speech as a satisfying whole, not just as a series of jokes and stories, however well they may have been crafted and structured.

The two **brackets** consist of a set-up at the opening of the speech and a pay-off at the end. The words you will end with include those planted clearly at the start. Many lyricists use the same trick, establishing a phrase at the start and repeating a variation of it to round off the last line. This how master songsmith Sammy Cahn achieved a nice little twist in the tail of 'Call Me Irresponsible':

Set-up: 'Call me irresponsible, call me unreliable, throw in undependable too.'

Pay-off: 'Call me irresponsible, yes I'm unreliable, but it's undeniably true: I'm irresponsibly mad for you.'

Brackets can serve you well in a speech, like this:

Set-up: 'Today, I confess, I've been daydreaming – both reminiscing about the past and predicting the future. We're celebrating a birthday, an anniversary. This society was founded exactly 20 years ago.'

Pay-off: 'At the end of my reminiscing, I've come to these conclusions. We have done much for this society . . . and this society has done much for us. Each and every one of us has good reason to be proud . . . and grateful. Let's congratulate ourselves and then move on to the next 20 years.'

Notice how the repetition of the words *reminiscing*, *society* and *20 years* helps the open-and-closed nature of the brackets and provides a pleasing symmetry. Do not simply repeat your opening. By all means use the same or very similar material, but give it some memorable and appropriate twist. It is vital that the argument has developed. Merely putting your audience back to where they started will give them the impression that you have wasted their time.

In this chapter, we rearranged Lewis Carroll's advice: we began with the middle, went on to the beginning and finished with the end of a speech. That's enough rabbit. As the King wisely counselled: it's time to stop.

QUESTIONS AND ANSWERS

I've been told to make my speech as long or as short as I wish. Can you offer any advice?
Don't suffer from the illusion that you can make your speech immortal by making it everlasting. If you have put together seven minutes of punchy and entertaining material, don't try to stretch it out for 12 minutes. A good seven-minute speech is far better than a dull 12-minute soliloquy. Your object is to entertain, not to put the audience to sleep. Leave them wanting more.

I've been known to suffer the occasional memory lapse. How can I prepare a speech which will help me deal with this problem?
Here is a simple method favoured by many speakers who fear 'drying up':

1. Write your speech out in *full* and number the pages.
2. *Memorise* the opening and closing lines and *familiarise* yourself with the remainder of the speech.
3. *Summarise* the speech on one card or one sheet of paper using *key words* to remind you of the *sequence* of jokes, anecdotes, quotations and so on, and make a note of the page numbers on which they appear. Attach the full speech to your summary.

The main advantage of this method is that you will cover everything you want to, give the impression of being natural and spontaneous and have the peace of mind that comes from knowing that in the last resort you can quickly use your full speech as a prompt if words fail you.

If you are *seriously* worried about your ability to stand and deliver, there is no point in giving yourself nightmares. Make an early and positive decision to *read* your script and then concentrate on giving variety and modulation to your reading voice. As you get into your speech, you will be pleasantly surprised how easy it becomes to ad lib and to raise your eyes from the printed page in order to establish and maintain that all-important contact you need to have with your audience.

SUMMARY

- A speech should not merely be an unconnected collection of jokes and stories. It needs to be properly structured.

- The texture of the speech should vary throughout, with a bias either towards one-liners or longer anecdotes, according to the nature and tastes of the audience.

- The whole thing should be an enjoyable journey through and over a series of valleys and peaks, with smooth transitions between friendly insults, genuine compliments, jokes and stories.

- It needs to begin with an appropriate hook that will grab your audience's attention and make them sit up and listen.

- You must end on a high note: humorous, thought-provoking, inspiring. As always, use whatever works.

- You can make a speech truly memorable by planting a bracket at the beginning and a matching one at the end.

6

Delivering Your Speech

Every communication is an opportunity to throw a bridge across a void. If you can do this, your speech will have more effect than you could ever have believed.

Essentially, you just need to be yourself – but *yourself made large*. You also need to learn a few tricks of the trade to enhance your natural platform skills. Until you know exactly what is going on – and why it's going on – you cannot be sure why parts of your speech are going down well while others may not be quite hitting the mark. You need to step back a little and take a broad view of the importance of:

- Finding your style.
- Giving out the right non-verbal messages.
- Acting your jokes out.
- Coping with nerves.

Only then can you decide what works for you – and what doesn't – and begin to develop a personal, unique and effective style of delivery.

FINDING YOUR STYLE

It is exceedingly difficult to discuss style and technique in general terms, since the ability to be entertaining and to tell jokes is such a personal business. However, there are certain 'rules' and guidelines which appear to be universal.

Making the speech 'yours'

If the same speech were presented by a million speakers, each and every version would be different. It is impossible *not* to make a speech uniquely yours. Did Elvis, Sinatra and Johnny Rotten all sound the same singing 'My Way'? Of course not.

The artist makes the crucial difference. So, too, does the speaker.

Most of the traditional advice on how to speak in public is out of date and, in many respects, it is wrong. True, a little judicious advice on open body language can smooth the edges without stifling individuality. And, as we shall see, an awareness of the chicken and egg nature of positive body language and positive attitudes to life generally can work wonders for you. Yet a great deal of so-called expert advice is counterproductive. Coaching does not work. Individual style is always the most effective style of communication for speakers, and is universally reassuring to audiences.

When you stand up to speak, you need to do three things.

- be conversational

- project your personality

- be heard.

These goals may sound glaringly obvious, yet few speakers even consider them.

Being conversational

When you are sitting leisurely, with family, friends or colleagues, your conversation will be naturally relaxed and chatty, because that is the language of easy communication. When you make an after dinner speech, the words and phrases you use should be more considered, imaginative, creative and rhythmical than your everyday language, yet the way you say them, the way you deliver your speech should remain unaffectedly relaxed and chatty.

If you are different from usual, you may be perceived as phoney, boring, or lacking in personality, so won't come over well. Certainly you may need to speak a little louder or make other concesssions to accommodate the needs of your audience, but, in essence, nothing in your delivery style should change. You should be yourself made large.

The key then is to recognise what you are doing when you 'get it right' and achieve *any* successful communication, be it formal or informal, business or social, and then stay with it. You need to recognise, and then capture, this normal style of communication and make it work for you, naturally, in any given situation, regardless of the stress level. When you walk into your office or a restaurant or a greengrocer's shop, you don't hover outside anxiously rehearsing how you will deliver your lines. We all communicate each day without fear of failure. If you can understand how normal, relaxed, informal spoken communication works, you will be able to understand what you must do, and keep on doing, during formal spoken communication.

So what are the critical elements of normal conversational communication which allow people to transmit and receive information effortlessly when they are relaxed and operating in a low-stress environment? Think about the differences between your casual conversation and the way you might deliver an after dinner speech.

The way you sound
Most of us are astonished the first time we hear our own voice. The resonant sounds we've heard in our heads seem thin and alien issuing from an audio or video player. It doesn't matter. Think about some of our top personalities, and most effective and entertaining communicators: Hancock, Lineker and Gower; Barker, McCoist and Parrott; Deayton, Hislop and Merton. None of these gifted talkers would win prizes at RADA. There is nothing of the mighty orator about any of them. All these famous and successful individuals stopped worrying about their voices long ago, if they ever did. They are each concerned with putting across their ideas in an entertaining manner. They speak to us with cheerfulness, cheeriness, vitality, vivacity – and occasionally conviction.

It doesn't matter whether speakers have accents which are unusual or even speech impediments, as long as people can *understand* them. Paradoxically, an unusual accent or speech problem can often help to reinforce a message by making it seem real and natural. From the moment you utter your famous first words you are testing different ways of catching people's attention and achieving what you want. All through your life you continue to build on these skills. Your conversational abilities are far more practised than your literary abilities. Casual conversation is not constructed in a literary way. You do not always finish your sentences. You repeat yourself. You use ungrammatical constructions – but you are obeying a different set of rules. You are obeying the rules of effective spoken communication which have been learnt, instinctively, down the ages. Don't abandon these rules when you speak in public.

Displaying your talents

Don't hide your light under a bushel. Any regional accents or dialects which you can do well (and only if you *can* do them well) should be incorporated into your stories. A punch line is doubled in effect in the appropriate Cockney or Brummie accent, besides giving you the chance to display yet another facet of your coruscating talents. However, be wary of mimicking the accents of racial minorities. As always, think very carefully about your audience and what they would laugh at and what they would find embarrassing and offensive.

Projecting your personality

Your personality is your greatest asset. It is personal chemistry that makes people want to associate with other people. Very few of us, given the choice, will choose to work or socialise with someone we don't like or trust. If you are already successful to any degree the chances are that you have a 'winning personality'. The challenge is to project it, not suppress it. If you succeed, you will feel comfortable and at ease. If you feel comfortable, your audience will feel comfortable and become receptive, open and focused. Mutual comfort is the key to successful communication.

Each speaker is unique; each speaker has a unique style. What might be most effective for one person would be a disaster for another. Think carefully about what *you* are doing when you communicate effortlessly under everyday circumstances. Probably you will not have considered this before. It is an extremely useful exercise because it makes you appreciate what you must also do during your speeches. In particular think about:

* the way you act

* the way you look.

The way you act

When a person talks informally, he probably sits or stands in a relaxed manner, breathing naturally, maintaining an appropriate level of eye contact, gesturing every now and then to reinforce his words, and smiling at intervals to establish and maintain rapport. Yet the moment this same person stands up to address an audience, he becomes nervous, distrusts his innate powers of communication and relies on a range of artificial presentation techniques.

We all want certainties to cling to when we are entering uncharted waters, which is why people visit astrologers – and speech trainers. I'll leave you to decide about astrologers, but much advice proffered by speech trainers is patently ludicrous: pushing your shoulders back throughout the speech; counting to six as you breathe in through your nose and to four as you push air out from the diaphragm; maintaining eye contact for at least 84% – yes 84% – of the presentation; exaggerating every gesture by one quarter; and smiling throughout. These are all genuine pieces of advice given by eminent trainers, and they are all very silly.

Certainly you should be aware of the importance of open body language generally. But once you begin to mimic gestures, the moment you are told to do something in a certain way, you become conscious of what you should be doing naturally. You have given yourself one more thing to think about, when all you should be thinking about is conveying the right message.

Whatever individual characteristics you have that are special to you should be nurtured and cultivated and worked on, for it is those personal and unique quirks of appearance, personality and expression that will mark you out as a speaker with something different to offer. And that is never a bad thing.

The way you look
Personal appearance has a major impact on how you are perceived by an audience. I would not presume to say any more about the way you dress or groom yourself, but would suggest you consider objectively what a powerful part of your assessment of others this is, and act appropriately.

Being heard
You must be *audible*. If you are not, all else is lost. If there is public address equipment available, find out how it works, get plenty of practice and then use it. Don't trust in luck and don't believe people who tell you to leave it all to them. Accept personal responsibility. You are the one who will look awkward if things go wrong.

If there is no sound-enhancing equipment, speak as clearly and as loudly as is necessary to be heard. If the only other person in the room was at the back, you would talk to him naturally, at the right level, without shouting or straining, by:

- keeping your head up
- opening your mouth wider than during normal speech
- using clearer consonants
- slowing down.

If you remember that you must be heard by that same man at the back during your speech, however many people may be in the room, you will make those same four *natural* adjustments to your delivery. However, and contrary to conventional wisdom, if you make a conscious effort to talk more slowly simply because you are in front of an audience, regardless of whether the farthest listener is 3 metres or 30 metres away, your delivery will sound unnatural and artificial. It doesn't matter whether you talk quickly or slowly, as long as you are speaking at the same rate as you would to talk only to that man at the back.

Getting back to basics

Once you accept that you can approach even the most daunting speech in exactly the same way as you approach informal communication, your apprehension will dwindle and your confidence will soar. Knowing that you not only *can*, but also *should* 'be yourself' will stop you worrying about your 'performance', and allow you to concentrate on what really matters: being yourself and entertaining your audience.

GIVING OUT THE RIGHT NON-VERBAL MESSAGES

If you abandon everything that is natural to you and substitute 'acquired' mannerisms when you rise to address an audience, you will come over as unnatural, awkward and insincere. However, this does *not* mean you should not attempt to project more open, positive body language. Far from it. This is not a contradiction. Your aim must be to make positive body language *natural* to you – natural throughout all your everyday encounters, not just whilst making speeches.

Once you begin to give out positive silent messages about your feelings and emotions, you will become even more enthusiastic and eager – and this will be reflected in your body language. You will have broken into a wonderful virtuous circle. Positive body language not only *reflects* positive feelings, it *creates* them.

What you must *never* do is attempt to put on an act when you speak in public. It will fool no one. Simply be aware of what is possible, give it a kick-start and then just let it happen. As actors are taught, you must: 'Dig deep to fly high and then throw it all away.'

Communicating with your whole body

We speak with vocal cords, but we communicate with our whole body. An audience does a lot more than just listen to a speech – it *experiences* it. Everything about a speaker's manner and demeanour contributes to the overall impression that the audience takes away. Body language is potent. When you address a group of people they are constantly responding consciously and unconsciously to what your body is saying to them.

All the main elements of body language – stance and posture, movement and gestures, and eye contact and facial expression – are immediately related and interdependent. You must send out an overall coordinated non-verbal message. And this message must also be consistent with your verbal message or you will lose all credibility. In the words of the old Chinese proverb: watch out for the man whose stomach does not move when he laughs.

It is not possible to successfully fake body language, but it is possible to learn how to project yourself far more positively, thereby showing your audience that you are:

- sincere
- enthusiastic
- natural
- friendly.

What hidden messages do you give out when you speak? If you are unsure, video yourself as you rehearse, or watch yourself in a mirror, or ask a kind but critical friend. You will probably find that you need to work on one or more of the following.

- stance and posture
- movement and gestures
- eye contact and facial expression.

However, remember that while each of these may be considered in isolation, a change made to any of them will also have a direct and immediate effect on the others.

Conveying confidence and integrity

Your stance and posture are important. You are making a fundamental statement with your body. An aligned, upright posture conveys a message of confidence and integrity. We can learn useful lessons from disciplines such as martial arts and various athletic activities in which participants cultivate a basic posture as a point of departure for all movement. In the same way you should aim to develop a basic posture for speaking.

Cultivating a basic posture

Stand upright with your feet shoulder-width apart and very slightly turned out. You can then shift your weight from one side to the other, if you have to, without being noticed. This simple posture is incredibly powerful – it projects confidence and power. A relaxed, upright posture suggests assurance; the opposite to sagging and slumping which suggests defeat. Audiences become more receptive and responsive when you stand before them calmly and with dignity. Keep well clear of the table though, leaning on it would make you look aggressive – and the tipple could easily topple.

Fig. 1. The caveman's aggressive body language.

This domineering stance is unsuitable for making an after dinner speech.

A friendly, upright, open, unthreatening stance is far preferable.

Fig. 2.   Don't threaten the audience!

Avoiding a threatening stance
Early man frightened his enemies by inflating his chest and spreading his arms to present a much wider profile (see Figure 1). Modern man uses exactly the same technique, consciously or unconsciously, when he wants to convince others of his dominance (see Figure 2).

Avoiding defensiveness
Our instincts tell us that people who shield themselves – even with just their arms – are defensive (see Figure 3), while people who do not shield themselves are perceived as open and friendly (see Figure 4).

Reinforcing your verbal messages
With an integrated basic posture as your point of departure, you are better able to realise your potential of communicating through movement. Awareness is the key to freeing yourself from unnecessary motion and it is best cultivated by watching yourself on video or a large mirror if video is unavailable. As your awareness increases so will your ability to leave out unwanted

Fig. 3. The defensive cavewoman.

Crossed arms are seen as
defensive and negative.

Open arms and open palms are
considered friendly and positive.

Fig. 4. Don't defend yourself against the audience!

Fig. 5. The hostile caveman.

movements and you will find it easier to move in a natural, expressive manner.

You should be far more than just a talking head. You don't want to be so motionless that you look like a statue on loan from Madame Tussaud's, but equally, you shouldn't attempt an impersonation of John McCririck's Saturday afternoon arm-waving histrionics – unless the story you are relating demands it. It is perfectly possible to make simple hand gestures which reinforce your verbal messages without distracting your audience. Avoid any movement or gesture that is likely to be seen as negative or inappropriate.

Avoiding hostile gestures
Early man attacked his victims by holding a weapon above their heads and bringing it down with great force (see Figure 5). Our legacy from this is that, even today, our ancestral memories perceive similar positions and movements as hostile (see Figure 6).

Identifying your bad habits
Do any of these faults apply to you?

Hands and fingers pointing upwards and finger-wagging, sweeping movements are seen as threatening.

Open palms with fingers downward are seen as unthreatening and friendly.

Fig. 6. Don't be hostile to the audience!

- playing with your watch
- talking with your hand in front of your mouth
- pushing your glasses back up your nose
- jingling coins in your pocket
- waving your hands about for no reason
- shuffling your feet
- swaying
- making pointless gestures.

Try to eliminate any such habits because they are a powerful means of distraction. Your audience will become preoccupied with when they will happen next and start watching you rather than listening to you.

Using your head
Eye contact and facial expression are crucial aspects of effective communication because they gain and then maintain an

audience's attention, create rapport, and give you valuable feed-back as to how well you are coming over. The worst you can do, apart from mumbling inaudibly, is not to look at your audience. Don't be ashamed to look at your script, but keep your head up as much as you can.

Maintaining eye contact
The eyes are – after words – the most powerful means of com-munication we possess. Sometimes a single glance can speak volumes. Eye contact is a humanising element in an often im-personal world. It is a crucial aspect in effective communication and thus an important part of every after dinner speech. Eye contact should be a simple, natural expression of your interest in the audience. It also allows you to monitor their level of interest in you. Making eye contact with your audience draws their atten-tion, helping them feel more personally involved.

Entertainers use the so-called **lighthouse technique** to maintain eye contact with their audiences. This means beaming all around the room slowly, tracing an imaginary X or Z shape but con-tinually varying the size and shape of the letter to avoid your eye sweeps becoming routine and predictable. Look at everyone and make this deliberate and noticeable. Stop occasionally to look at individuals for just long enough to give the impression that you are talking to them without picking them out for special attention.

Conveying emotion
You must do more than simply look at your audience; you must also use your eyes and your facial expression to convey emotion. This isn't as difficult as it may sound. You do it every day. Practise using your eyes and facial expression to convey: happiness, surprise, optimism, mirth, joy, love, confidence, sincerity.

Smiling
There is nothing more captivating than a smile. Smilers are thought of as warm, outgoing people while those who restrict this expression are perceived as cold and withdrawn. The expression on your face can actually dramatically alter your feelings and perceptions. Deliberately smiling or frowning can create the corresponding emotional responses. Remember that openness and smiles are winners. So smile, smile – and smile again!

Captivating your audience
The effectiveness of your speech will depend, to a large extent, on how you look and sound. A relaxed stance and upright posture, purposeful economy of movement and fluid gestures, lively eyes and facial expression, and expressive voice, will all capture your audience's attention and greatly enhance the impact of your speech.

Not putting on an act
The key, then, is to recognise the importance of projecting yourself positively and to have the self-confidence to break into that virtuous circle of positive body language and genuine positive feelings and emotions. You will be amazed how each element will reinforce the other. By all means practise to find the best ways to get your jokes and stories across, but as you rise to address your audience, relax and allow your natural winning personality to be projected through your now natural open body language.

Displaying an audience awareness
Body language is a two-way street. A speaker must not only know what messages he is *conveying*; he must also be able to read and react to the non-verbal feedback he is continuously *receiving* from his audience.

If the audience were sitting back in their seats with their chins down and arms crossed a perceptive speaker would get the message that his speech was not getting across. He would become aware that he needed to take a different approach to gain the audience's involvement, or cut straight to his close. A non-perceptive speaker would blunder on regardless.

Looking for gesture clusters
Like any other language, body language consists of words, sentences and punctuation. Each gesture is like a single word, and a word may have several different meanings. It is only when you put words into sentences that you can fully understand its meaning. Gestures come in sentences.

One of the most serious mistakes a speaker can make is interpreting a solitary gesture in isolation. That man at the back may be sitting cross-legged not because he is negative or hostile but because he suffers from arthritis. And that woman may have her arms tightly crossed simply because she is cold. The man in the corner may be continually looking towards the door not because he wants to go home but rather because he's still hoping he hasn't been stood up.

However, if one person is displaying *all* these gestures: sitting cross-legged, arms tightly crossed, continually looking towards the door, the odds are he does not like what he is hearing. And if everyone in the room is mirroring these gesture patterns, you are in trouble! Take another approach or cut straight to your close.

ACTING YOUR JOKES OUT

There are fundamental differences in written, spoken and visual humour. To illustrate this let's consider how a story can improve in the **telling** and **showing** over the bald facts on the printed page.

Suppose you want to tell the guests about your drinking habits. Use the fact that you are on your feet to your advantage. Begin with a couple of general one-line gags about boozing to get the laughs flowing before relating a story which you can **act out**. For example, you might say:

'Do you know, in this town there are more than 350 pubs. But I can tell you that I haven't been in one of them. Problem is I can never remember which one of them I haven't been in.

'I drank so much on our trip to Europe last summer that when we got to Italy I was the only one in the party who couldn't see anything wrong with the Tower of Pisa. And I was so drunk when we came back that they had to pay duty on me to get me through Customs. I don't just drink to excess . . . I drink to anything.

'But apparently things have got to change – she who must be obeyed has decreed it. Last week she found a case of whisky hidden in the kitchen and told me to empty each and every bottle down the sink, or else . . . so last Saturday I reluctantly proceeded with the unhappy task.

'I drew the cork from the first bottle and poured the contents down the sink, with the exception of a glass, which I drank.

'Then I pulled the cork from a second bottle and did likewise, with the exception of another glass, which I consumed.

'I emptied the third bottle, except another glass, which I drank and then took the cork from the fourth sink, poured the glass down the bottle and drank that too.

'I pulled the bottle from the next glass, I drank a sink out of it, and emptied the rest down the cork.

'Then I pulled the sink from the next bottle and poured it down the glass and I drank the cork, and finally I took glass from the last bottle, emptied the cork, poured the sink down the rest and drank the pour.

'When I had emptied everything, I steadied the house with one hand, counted the bottles and glasses and corks with the other and found there were 31.

'To make sure, I recounted them when they came by again and this time there were 72.

'As the house came around the next time I counted them again, and finally I had all the houses and sinks and glasses and corks and bottles counted, except one house, which I then drank.'

Obviously the humour would be greatly enhanced if you acted out the story and included a few relevant movements, gestures, expressions, slurs and stumbles as you become more and more inebriated.

The precise wording and style of delivery of a joke or story, of course, is *yours*, not mine. But I hope this simple example will encourage the novice to look at his material a little more carefully to see what can be extracted over and above the obvious punch line reaction.

Being inclusive

It is in the nature of after dinner speaking that you will find the quickest response from the front of the nearest tables, but don't ignore the poor folks at the back who will feel more and more alienated if you appear to be having a private party with your mates down at the front. Give everyone the benefit of your big blue eyes and flashing smile every once in a while.

Keeping it short

If you are asked to speak for 15 minutes, sit down after 12. If things are not going well, cut straight to your close; and even if you feel you're wowing them, don't make the mistake of out-staying your welcome. Quit while you're ahead. Follow the example of the man who was asked to give a talk on the subject of sex. 'It gives me great pleasure', he said, and he sat down.

Learning from the novelist

Let your story have a hero – and make this person someone they can identify with. If possible, make it someone they know – and preferably someone who is in the room. Don't just say, 'A friend of mine had an interesting experience last week. He was in Birmingham when . . .'. Say instead, 'Alan Wall, – you all know him – there he is hiding at the back. Anyway, Alan tells me he was in Birmingham last week when he had an interesting experience . . .'

Learning from the bar-stool joker

'An Englishman, an Irishman and a Scotsman were on an aeroplane . . .'. The bar-stool joker does not describe the trio. His listeners do not ask the destination of the flight. Similarly, you should leave out *unnecessary* detail and permit the fertile mind of each individual in your audience to supply the little touches of colour. Recognise the power of their imaginations, and let it work for you. Be economical. Keep it crisp. Give them the framework but leave it to them to draw the picture – and to colour it in:

> 'We went to Greece last summer . . . Had the shish kebabs all week.'

Learning from the stand-up comic

Stand-up comics frequently deliver their material in what is known as the 'dramatic present':

> 'So here I am, waiting for my bus in the High Street. It is pouring it down and this bloke shouts out to me from a passing car . . .'

The use of the present tense – *am, pouring it down, shouts out* – gives it a sense of immediate excitement. Your audience will feel an enlivened change of tempo if you do the same.

Starting a joke

You should start a joke as the laughter from the previous gem dies down; not too soon or you won't be heard, and not too late or your speech will begin to drag. But what is that precise moment? Experience will tell you which lines get long laughs and which mere titters. For the titters, you need not wait at all; for the surefire barnstormers, there is often a moment when the laughter fades – and then rises up afresh.

You can either pick that moment, thus keeping the speech flowing at the possible expense of muffing the impact of your next gag, or you can help the laugh along by **corpsing**, not in the sense of forgetting your lines, but rather by beginning to laugh yourself with a kind of 'yes, that was a good one, wasn't it?' expression. If an audience has really split its sides over a gag, they will always enjoy the speaker's appreciation of their mirth. But don't laugh at your own jokes *too* often.

Maintaining the momentum
By linking material, you help to give a speech continuity and establish the illusion that you are chatting informally, with the laughs emerging almost incidentally. Don't make your links *too* tenuous. On *The Morning Line*, Derek Thompson once linked some old hoofage of the great 1960s steeplechaser Arkle with news about that afternoon's race-card. He said, 'Well, Arkle won't be running today – and here are today's other non-runners.' Actually, that link was so awful it had a charm of its own. But he wouldn't have got away with too many more like that!

If you are topping a laugh on a previous joke it is often worthwhile to repeat or rephrase the first words of a story. This ensures there are no dead-spots and that the plot of the next joke is understood. For instance:

'I wouldn't say she's been a bad girl but . . .'
(*As the laughter from the previous joke dies down.*)

'No, she hadn't really been a bad girl but—'
(*If one person is still laughing*)

'Have you just worked it out?'
(*Pause*)

'Well, put it back, I wouldn't say she'd . . .'
(*Pause for laughter*)

'No, come on, we've got a lot to get through, and I want to get home before the pills wear off . . . No she hadn't been a bad girl . . . but they buried her in a Y-shaped coffin.'

Timing

Timing is such a delicate and elusive art that definition, instruction or advice are impossible. It is instinctive – though it is also a gift that can be improved with practice. Timing depends ultimately on your style. Both quick-fire delivery and slow burn are valid techniques; whether one or the other or something in between is right for you, only you can decide.

Finishing a joke

Bang out your punch line with clarity and confidence – and wait. If there is a stony silence, don't compound the potential embarrassment by making a boring crack like, 'Is this an audience or a jury?' If the **bummer** was a one-liner, they probably didn't even realise that it *was* a joke. Just move on – and quickly. Let your charm and warmth break them down, even if your material hasn't – so far.

Laugh and the world won't laugh with you

Don't be shy about laughing at your own jokes *occasionally* – it bonds you with your audience. However, don't do it too often or you'll come over as over-confident and self-congratulatory. For the most part allow your audience to discover how funny you are for themselves. And *never* laugh until you've finished the gag. You may know the punch line is going to be hilarious, but your audience won't – until they've heard it!

Reacting to laughs

Generally, the best reaction to laughs is an appreciative smile and a slick manoeuvre into your next line. However, here are a few stock phrases you could use in response to their response to you:

Big laugh

'For two pins I'd tell it again . . .'

'I'd tell you more like that, but you'd only laugh.'

(*After a risqué story*) '(Prudish female character) told me that one.'

Small laugh

'I'm glad you both came.'

'Was it something I said?'

'So this is where the good jokes come to die.'

Single laugh
   'No solo titters, please.'

   'It's you and me against the rest.'

   'Pass it on.'

Late laugh
   'Would you mind laughing with the others, sir, or they'll think I'm working you with my foot.'

   'Hello – he's woken up!'

   'You must be a late developer.'

No laugh
Move on! Don't make things worse. The following one-liners should be used with extreme caution and only when you are *sure* that the audience is on your side even though they're not laughing very much.

   'That was my e-mail joke . . . you should have got it straight away.'

   'Me English . . .'

   'My mother told me there would be nights like this.'

Fluffing a joke
Don't worry if you mess up a line or two. Quite frankly, the audience won't give a damn. The worst think you can do is to become embarrassed because then *they* will become embarrassed for you. This is not a turning point in Western civilisation. The world will continue unimpeded tomorrow. Just laugh it off:

   'That's the last time I get my teeth by mail order.'

   'Sorry, I'm breaking these teeth in for my dog.'

   'All the right words . . . but not necessarily in the right order.'

Putting it all together

Always consider how you can bring a story to life through your natural actions and reactions, as well as your words. Remember that an audience watches you as well as listens to you. Keep a strong impetus in your delivery and in pauses between jokes – that first contact with your audience must never be broken. This effort of concentration, or erecting and maintaining a psychic bridge between yourself and your audience, is the reason why successful speakers often finish bathed in sweat. It isn't the heat from the lights or the physical exertion involved, it is the sheer outpouring of self, of spirit, of that dynamism which excites attention and evokes affection.

COPING WITH NERVES

Fear is nothing to be frightened of. People get nervous because they are afraid of failing, of looking foolish, and not living up to expectations. Nervousness is caused by the fear of looking ridiculous to others. Few speakers claim to be able to speak with no nerves. Some will say that lack of nerves is not only unlikely, it is undesirable. They need the adrenaline to carry them along. So how do you make things easier for yourself? First be assured that worry is avoidable. The greatest antidote to it is preparation.

Preparation

You must allow yourself plenty of time to prepare. If you don't have the time to do yourself justice don't accept a speaking engagement. Once you have gathered, switched or devised your own material and structured your speech, it's time to **rehearse** it.

Rehearsing

Friends who tell you not to worry should worry you. Don't believe them when they say, 'No need to rehearse, it'll be alright on the night' – unless your hidden agenda is to get £250 from Lisa Riley for a camcorder calamity. If you want to calm your nerves and make a great speech, you simply *must* rehearse.

As with the type of script you use, so the rehearsal method you employ must be the one that best suits you. Some speakers like to be isolated and unheard in a distant room, with or without a mirror. Others perform their speeches again and again to a sympathetic spouse or friend, either encouraging suggestions from them or requiring nothing more than a repeated hearing to ease away inhibitions.

Rehearse your opening and close until you have got them spot on. Rehearse the body of your speech not to be *perfect*, but to be *comfortable*. Audiences don't care if you're perfect, but they will only be comfortable if you are. And if they are not comfortable, they will not be receptive.

If you get the chance of a run-through at the actual location of the dinner, grasp it, especially if you will be using a mike. And you'll find it extremely useful to get a feel for the place and to become familiar with the layout of the room.

You'll also find that repeated practice is often the best way to recognise the parts of your speech that hit the mark, the parts that require a little fine-tuning, and the parts that are simply not worth including.

Fighting first-night fright
Why do some actors freeze or fumble on the opening night and then pick up a British Theatre Drama Award six months later? It's a fear of unfamiliarity. As the days, weeks and months go by, the fear abates and the quality of the performance improves. Therefore the more rehearsal, the more the certainty of success and greater peace of mind. Words become more familiar. Awkward juxtapositions are smoothed out. You suddenly think of a way of saying a stuffy sentence in a more straightforward and colloquial style.

Making it real
Whatever form of rehearsal you favour, in private or with a companion, try to reproduce in your mind the circumstances of your final performance. Until you practise thinking and speaking aloud on your feet, you haven't rehearsed what will actually happen.

Warming up

The big day has arrived. Warming up will help you transform fear and its accompanying stiffness and tension into power and poise. All too often speakers ready themselves like condemned prisoners approaching the walk to the gallows. They sit rigid, imagining every possible fearful eventuality. Instead of sitting and worrying find a place where you can move freely and practise the following exercises.

Becoming aware of your breathing
Concentrate on the rhythm and flow of your breathing without trying to change it. Do this for 30 seconds. Then allow yourself a deep full inhalation followed by an extended complete exhalation. Do this five times allowing each breath to be deeper than the one before. To enhance the effectiveness of this further make a deep sighing *ahhhh* sound as you exhale. This simple exercise is very powerful and relaxing. It will help you feel calm and energised at the same time.

Opening your voice
However strong and free your voice is you cannot just stand up and expect it to be there for you. Just as any good speaker will take a few minutes before they begin going over their script, so you should also check out that voice.

If possible have five minutes of voice warm-up in the loo or in a private room. It is a bit like a concert artist warming up his musical instrument. Experiment with yawning, sighing and humming. Sing vowel sounds in descending and ascending scales without straining. Discover your highest and lowest note. You can even practise singing the first few minutes of your speech. These simple exercises will help prevent you choking up as they will enhance the quality and resonance of your voice.

Waking up your eyes
Hold your index finger, the shiny tip of a pen or the beam of a pocket torch in front of your eye and move it around keeping your eyes focused on the object. Move it at random to the limits of your visual fields. Do this as quickly as you can without moving your head. Practise for 20 to 30 seconds. This exercise will wake up your eyes. When they are alive, bright and clearly focused so are you.

Vocalising your face
Take a minute, in front of a mirror if possible, and make as many different faces as you can – happy, sad, angry, stupid, surprised, frightened. Hold each expression for about five seconds. Warming up your face in this manner allows you to feel more open and permits a greater range of expressions.

Visualising success

As you practise these warm-up exercises you will find your fear and stiffness transformed into enthusiasm and freedom. Reinforce these feelings with a positive visualisation of your speech. Imagine yourself talking in a relaxed and confident manner. You are looking good. They love your opening hook. But it gets better; your stories and jokes wow them. They are eating out of your hand. Then comes that big finish. Nobody could have topped that. Listen to their cheers and applause. Now that's what I call an after dinner speech! Let your energy flow. What you used to call fear can now be re-named excitement and anticipation.

Thinking audience

Focus primarily on your audience and their needs, not on yourself. Excess nervousness and self-consciousness feed off each other in a vicious circle. When nervous we tend to focus too much on ourselves and our weaknesses. This negative focus creates more nervousness, and so on. Alternatively, if you keep your attention focused on the needs of your audience and on your commitment to fulfilling your objectives you won't have time or cause to worry.

Always remember that your audience *wants* you to succeed. They are not a jury. Your audience is made up of individuals not unlike yourself. Tell yourself that you will not be intimidated. You have been invited to take command of the moment. Grasp the opportunity with both hands.

Finally, most audiences have been habituated to a very low standard of after dinner speech. People are regularly exposed to lifeless, unimaginative talks which seem to drone on interminably. Because you care enough about excellence to have read this far you will undoubtedly rise well above the average audience's expectations.

QUESTIONS AND ANSWERS

I've heard it said that a speaker's performance begins long before he speaks. Is this true?

Yes, too many speakers seem to think they can only be seen when they stand and deliver. This isn't the case. If you slurp your soup, spill peas all over the floor and ignore your neighbour's valiant attempts at making polite conversation, the audience will notice.

It's no good becoming good Dr Jekyll when you stand up; your audience will have already seen nasty Mr Hyde.

What can I do if I get a sudden attack of the collywobbles in the few moments before I'm due to speak?
Remind yourself that this is a happy occasion. The audience is on your side. They are willing you to do well. But if the pressure is still getting to you, try this emergency relaxation technique:

1. Pull in your stomach muscles tightly. Relax.
2. Clench your fists tightly. Relax.
3. Extend your fingers. Relax.
4. Grasp the seat of your chair. Relax.
5. Press your elbows tightly into the side of your body. Relax.
6. Push your feet into the floor. Relax.

What should I do if I feel I am losing control of my voice during my speech?
Don't panic! If you feel yourself speeding up, stop and take a couple of deep breaths. That will slow you down. If you feel you're getting hoarse, then take a drink of water. That has the effect of cooling the back of your throat. If you feel your voice getting higher as you speak, once again take a drink of water. That will enable your voice box to drop down as you swallow, and that, in turn, will help to bring your voice down.

SUMMARY

- Find your own style of delivery.

- Don't hide your talents under a bushel.

- Break into the virtuous circle of positive body language.

- Don't just tell gags – act them out.

- Fear is nothing to be frightened about.

- Rehearse. A speech is like a pair of shoes: it will always benefit from a little more polishing.

7

Top Tips from Professional Speakers

Finally, here are some words of advice from some of the best speakers on today's professional after dinner circuit. They don't always agree with one another. And why should they? That would remove the wonderfully imperfect distinctions about them – and us – and help create a world of unremarkable clones. Think carefully about all their tips and then decide which ones would work best for *your* speech – and for *you*.

ADVICE FROM A SPEAKER AGENCY

First though, what qualities do speaker agencies look for in after dinner speakers? Aveline Hughes, Public Relations Co-ordinator for Celebrity Speakers Limited, which represents such international illuminati as F. W. De Klerk, Helmut Schmidt and Baroness Thatcher, explains.

Celebrity Speakers Limited

All successful speeches follow certain tried and tested guidelines relating to content, structure, delivery and attitude. A combination of all these qualities and skills *always* results in a memorable and outstanding after dinner speech. A speech that does *not* have the right balance of these qualities and skills will not leave an audience with a lasting impression.

Speech content
The information in the speech must be relevant to the particualar audience addressed and relevant to the particular event in question. The age, status, gender, cultural level, education, nationality, interests, motivations and expectations of the audience must be taken into consideration when thinking about what will be said in the speech.

The audience should always be able to relate to the content. A successful speaker always delivers theory in a language his audience can understand without being patronising and without overwhelming those present with technical jargon. Including the right balance of humour and seriousness is another essential element when considering the content of a speech.

Speech structure
The message and theme should be crystal clear to the audience within the first three minutes of the speech. The line of argument or thread should run throughout the speech and lead to a strong conclusion. The ideas developed should be substantiated with examples or anecdotes.

Delivery of speech
A successful speaker will be eloquent, he will have a fluent delivery and use a linguistic register appropriate to the academic level of the audience. A good speaker always projects his voice upwards and out towards his audience while maintaining constant contact with everyone he is addressing. An audience should feel they are being spoken to not spoken at.

Attitude
Outstanding speakers are always charismatic and have a natural ability to connect with and captivate an audience. Not everyone is born with these qualities; however, a positive, professional and cooperative attitude all contribute to delivering a successful speech.

ADVICE FROM WELL-KNOWN SPEAKERS

Gyles Brandreth
(Broadcaster, writer and former After Dinner Speaker of the Year)
I offer four quick reminders:

Be aware
Be aware of what you want to achieve. What message do you want to convey? What impact do you want to make? Remember that what you want to hear yourself say may not be what your audience wants to hear. Be aware of what you want, but be as keenly aware of what they want too. Once you have decided on the goal of your speech, make sure nothing within it deflects from that end. Will each passage produce the right kind of buzz in at

least one key element of your audience? If it doesn't it's a waste of words.

Be brief
No one has ever complained because a speech was too brief. It's always better to leave them wanting more and always better to cut much-loved paragraphs in their entirety than gabble through it all at break-neck speed. When speaking, take your time, particularly at the beginning. When you stand, pause, take in the room, wait for the hush (yes, wait-for-as-long-as-it-takes) before you start.

Be prepared
For me, total audience awareness requires a totally clear head. Not drinking before speaking is one rule that in more than 30 years of what feels like non-stop spouting, I've never broken.

Unless you are accustomed to scripting speeches, a written text will sound like an essay, which is why I recommend notes rather than written script. Write them on cards and number the cards, just in case they fall to the floor the moment before you are due on your feet.

If you are offered a microphone, use it. People will think they can hear you better if you are standing in front of it. And if it's on while you're speaking make sure it's off before you sit back after your oration and mutter to your neighbour that the audience were a bunch of fools but it seemed to go okay none the less.

Be bold
Dare to be yourself. Don't tell jokes if it's not your style. Don't be formal if you are not inclined. Go as far as you want to go in whatever direction, making sure you are taking the audience with you as you go. Follow your instincts. Picasso did not paint bunches of flowers.

Tony Ball
(Marketeer, businessman and former Business Speaker of the Year)
Prepare, pretend to be confident and always flatter the audience. Use humour, use notes and use your hands. Smile and weave stories around the appropriate characters present and exude a friendly sincerity. Be natural, be topical and only drink during toasts. Emphasise in threes, as I am doing here. Include a brief serious message, don't pick your nose – and pray.

Ivor Spencer
(Professional toastmaster, Toastmaster of the Year 2000)
Do not accept an engagement unless you have the time to write specifically for the occasion. Write more than they need and then edit it. Then either read from the speech using double spacing so it will be clear in case you lose your place, or instead of writing a speech, have some headings written down which will remind you of what you want to say.

If you are an amateur, then from my experience of listening to over 50,000 speeches, which has been mentioned in *The Guinness Book of Records*, speak for no more than five minutes. A professional speaker can usually speak for 15 to 45 minutes. The important maxim to understand is to leave the guests wanting more.

Professor Laurie Taylor
(Academic, broadcaster and writer)
Anyone can make a successful after dinner speech. The key is to project your unique personality, punch your full weight, show off and enjoy yourself. Stand up slowly and modestly. Use plenty of eye contact. Bring them all in. Don't allow anyone to outstare you. Either gesture fully or don't gesture at all; there can be no half-way house. Don't use notes. Just familiarise yourself with your speech. Actors can learn most parts within two weeks and even play *Hamlet* within five. A short after dinner speech should present no difficulties. But be prepared to improvise. Live dangerously.

Dickie Bird
(Former cricket umpire and writer)
It's a bit like being an umpire. Drill down deep. Find out what there is on the *in*side, that should be on the *out*side. Be true to yourself. Be open. Be honest. Don't rest behind shyness, false modesty or lack of thought. Share your emotions. Speak to people on a one-to-one basis, however large your audience. All communication must be personal. It may need to be 'multi-personal', but it should never be 'mass'. Good speechmaking is presenting yourself well – not putting on a show.

Sir Ranulph Fiennes
(Explorer and writer)
If you are going to give a talk to a luncheon or dinner at a

conference, make sure the organisers have told the audience that at the end of the meal there is going to be a speaker. You might think they always do, but they don't.

Very often the audience – which might be a couple of hundred jaded businessmen – who have just had two days of in-house lecturing – are expecting that as soon as their last night's dinner is over they can go to the bar or catch a taxi into town. If they are now told that they have to listen to someone they have probably never heard of on a subject they might think totally unrelated to their conference, you are onto a loser straight away. So my big tip is: make sure that the organisers have told the audience that there is going to be a speech after the meal.

Lord Cowdrey of Tonbridge
(Writer and former cricketer)
Enjoy the occasion, apply a gentle touch. Never apologise but remain modest. A serious pearl of wisdom in a sandwich of two appropriate funnies works wonderfully well. Mind your language and leave blue stories to the masters of that way of life. Keep it short. If they ask for 20 minutes, sit down after 18.

Rachel Heyhoe Flint
(Public relations and sports marketing consultant, journalist, broadcaster and sportswoman)
Always prepare your speech; no two audiences are the same even though the theme may be the same from your point of view. Get advance information about your client/top table/guests/audience so that you can make it feel as though you know them personally.

Always be on time; meet your hosts beforehand so that you can confirm their requirements. Try the microphone out in advance if possible and look for hidden perils in the room. If you have the choice, speak from a table with your back to the wall so you can view all the audience.

Don't worry if you are a little nervous, worry if you are not. Never drink before delivery so that you have your wits about you all the time. Be prepared for chat-back with a few gentle put-downs ('I apologise if I'm interrupting while you are speaking!'). If you have to write notes, type them boldly on a card so that your nerves don't make the papers in your hand tremble like a willow tree in the breeze. Headings are better than full sentences for anecdotes because you will tell them more naturally.

Warm the audience as soon as possible with an amusing opener (unless you are speaking at a funeral!). Don't outstay your welcome. Sense if your audience have had enough and want to get to the bar.

Professor Patrick Minford
(Academic and writer)
Try to understand your audience and its particular interests, mood and background. What is expected of you? Some speakers are stand-up comics, some are serious, some are soothing and congratulatory. Even if you are at the serious end, then you still need some humour. This allows people to get their breath between bits of serious content and helps them feel more relaxed about the whole thing.

For economists (and most people) jokes that are relevant (and they should be if possible) are hard to come by. For this reason formulaic jokes are useful (for example, statesman crossing crocodile-infested river fends off crocodile with tee-shirt saying something outrageous about policy or business or whatever: punch line – not even a crocodile would swallow that). Finally, don't worry if a few people have heard you and your jokes before. It just can't be helped and they usually will enter into the spirit.

Barry Took
(Broadcaster and writer)
After you have been introduced, stand silently for five seconds. It will seem like an age but it gives the audience a chance to settle and for you to relax. Try whenever possible to start with some reference to the room, the occasion or the meal. Flatter your hosts: 'the best meal', 'the nicest people', 'such wonderful company' and so on.

All speeches should be autobiographical: 'As a deep sea diver I have had many interesting experiences. I remember a shark I met . . .'. If you stick to what you know, you won't go far wrong. If it's going badly, wind up and sit down. Only tell jokes if you know how.

Heather Couper
(Science broadcaster and writer)
For someone who enjoys wine (especially antipodean) as much as I do, I'd advise going cautiously on the Shiraz, even though everyone else is going gently legless. And find out as much as you

can about key personnel in advance (a tip that came to me via the late Roy Castle). You'll feel more bonded to them; they'll appreciate your efforts; and everyone – you and the audience – will experience a much more personal occasion.

Ian McCaskill
(Former weather forecaster)
Stay sober. As a confirmed boozer, I can tell you that the only fragile edge you have over those bright people out there is that you can be sober whilst they are not. Never use notes. Remember that your audience have no idea what you are going to say, nor the order. If you miss out your best joke, too bad.

Teresa Gorman
(Member of Parliament and writer)
Be natural and topical. Tell plenty of anecdotes, especially ones against yourself. People often come to weigh up what kind of person you are as much as to hear what you have to say. Try to go round and talk to each table so that everyone thinks they have met you personally. Then they'll go home and tell their friends what a nice person you are!

Charles Kennedy
(Member of Parliament, Leader of the Liberal Democrats, broadcaster and writer)
I have always taken the view that the best style of after dinner speech is to begin on a humorous note and end on a slightly more serious one. That way people will feel that they have been entertained whilst at some point left with something to reflect upon. And keep it about 15–20 minutes in length.

Tony Benn
(Member of Parliament, writer and inaugural Channel 4 Parliamentary Speaker of the Year)
It is sincerity rather than oratory that defines a great speech – when what someone's saying is rooted in his life and convictions – sincerity, and in a funny way modesty.

Lord Janner of Braunstone
(Barrister, broadcaster, lecturer, journalist and writer)
Always prepare a fall back. I always prepare serious material as a back up. If the jokes don't go, then I turn serious. It is almost

certainly not what the audience wants – after dinner audiences require above all to be entertained. But it is better than the alternative – a disaster of humour failed.

Sir John Harvey-Jones
(Businessman, trouble-shooter and writer)
The ideal after dinner speech is no more than 12 minutes long and a successful one involves keeping the audience laughing for at least eight minutes. You should also include one or two salient and appropriate business or other points.

Harvey Thomas
(International public relations consultant)
Here are my Ten Commandments:

- See yourself as *others* see you.

- Have specific *objectives* for each communication.

- Have an overall *picture/message* in mind – *before* you start on details.

- Work out the *route plan* for your speech.

- Make it *easy*. Lead your audience along. *Headline. Signpost.*

- *Rehearse.* But don't memorise.

- Win *hearts*, then minds. Win the *person* – not the argument. *Attitude* persuades best.

- Keep it *simple.*

- Be *enthusiastic.*

- Be *yourself.*

Sir Peter Ustinov
(Actor, dramatist, film director and raconteur)
Advice to would-be after dinner speakers? I would say that, in order to take them by surprise – and surprise is an essential ingredient in good speaking, as it is in military strategy and in love – it is imperative to take risks, by taking yourself by surprise. Don't rehearse too meticulously. Don't learn things by heart – and certainly not other people's poetry. 'I think it was Kipling who once said . . .' and so on. He probably didn't, and if he did, he shouldn't have.

The main thing is to have a point of view, and to release your imagination in the parkland of your subject, like a dog. Then, as the dog does, rely on instinct. Don't go on for too long. If the public is wonderful, stop a little short of total triumph. Also resist the temptation to laugh at your jokes before reaching the point. The audience may find this inhibiting, to the point of not wishing to join in the laughter, your laughter. There are many rules, but, as usual, they are there only to be broken.

There you have it in a nutshell from some of the best after dinner speakers in the world. It would be impertinent of me to add anything except to thank them on your behalf. I do so, most warmly.

Appendix 1
Etiquette and All That

Take a look at the menu to confirm the pattern of the evening ahead of you. The usual order of speeches at a formal do is as follows.

The loyal toast
The toastmaster bangs on the table and proposes the toast to Her Majesty the Queen. This may be followed by the simultaneous ignition of matches and lighters accompanied by an evening chorus of spluttering and coughs.

The toast to the society
If the occasion involves a society, someone will talk about its history and discuss some issue of current interest to the audience.

The Chairperson's response
The chairperson makes his contribution to the evening – often at length.

The toast to the ladies and guests
One of your hosts names the top table guests, saving you, as principal speaker, for last.

Being introduced
Always have someone introduce you. Never introduce yourself, even if you are well known to every person in the room. And don't leave the wording of the announcement to chance. Write a short, crisp introduction and hand it to the M.C. to read out. Firmly yet politely make it abundantly clear that the audience should *not* be told that you provided your own intro. Otherwise he is likely to use the fact to get a cheap laugh – and at *your* expense:

'It isn't often that I have the pleasure of introducing a truly great after dinner speaker – and tonight is no exception. Please welcome . . .'

'I'm not going to stand around and bore you with a lot of pathetic old jokes. Instead, I'm going to introduce a man who can do that much better than I can . . .'

'A man like our guest speaker is certainly hard to find. Tonight, for instance, we had to look in three pubs and a wine bar. But we found him. Please put your hands together to welcome . . .'

Your response

It's showtime! When the final applause has died down, the chair-person may complete the proceedings with a vote of thanks. And so to bed.

Appendix 2
Addressing Titled People

If the occasion is formal, correct titles and forms of address should be equally formal, even if you consider them pompous. To ignore them on those grounds is to invite ridicule because, unless you explain your reasons for ignoring accepted form, your audience will merely think you are ignorant.

ROYALTY DOESN'T TAKE PRECEDENCE

It is important to get it right. First on your list of the rich and good must be the person in the chair: 'Mr Chairman', 'Madam Chairman', 'Mr President' or 'Madam President'. Next comes any royal who may have dropped in: 'Your Majesty' (for the Queen or the Queen Mother) or 'Your Royal Highness' (for any other member of the Royal Family). Third comes anyone else present whom you consider worthy of a special mention: 'Madam Mayor', 'Lady Penelope', 'Canon Gunn'. Fourth comes the person to whose speech you are replying: 'Mr Jones', 'Mrs Smith'. Finally, comes the catch-all 'My Lords, Ladies and Gentlemen'. In practice, of course, your roster is more likely to include perhaps three or four individuals and groups, but five is a possibility:

'Madam Chairman, Your Royal Highness, Mr Mayor, Miss Moneypenny, My Lords, Ladies and Gentlemen . . .'

ADDRESSING OTHER HIGH-UPS

The following is not meant to be an exhaustive list of titles, but it does contain those most often encountered. You'll find a comprehensive list at your local library. Ask to see either a copy of *Debrett's Correct Form* or *Debrett's Etiquette and Modern Manners* or A & C Black's *Titles and Forms of Address*. If a titled guest is unexpectedly present at the gathering, ask the toastmaster what the form is. No one will think the less of you for having to ask, and to do so will save embarrassment all round.

The Peerage

Baron	Lord XXX
Baroness	Lady XXX
Duke	My Lord Duke, or Your Grace
Duchess	Your Grace
Marchioness	My Lady Marchioness
Marquis	My Lord Marquis
Viscount	My Lord Viscount
Viscountess	My Lady Viscountess

Central Government

Backbenchers	By name
Chancellor of the Exchequer	By appointment or by name
The Lord Chancellor	The Lord Chancellor
The Lord Chief Justice	The Lord Chief Justice
Ministers	Minister, or by name
Prime Minister	Mr/Madam Prime Minister
Secretaries of State	By appointment or by name

Local Government

Chairman	Mr/Madam Chairman
Councillor	Councillor XXX
Lady Mayoress	My Lady Mayoress
Lord Mayor	My Lord Mayor, or Your Worship
Mayor	Mr/Madam Mayor, or Your Worship
Provost	My Lord Provost

A female Lord Mayor is not to be confused with a Lady Mayoress. The former should be addressed as 'My Lord Mayor'. Sexist it may be, but that's the way it is. The latter is the female consort of the Lord Mayor, and should be addressed as 'My Lady Mayoress'.

Clerical titles

Archbishop	Your Grace
Archdeacon	Mr Archdeacon, or Archdeacon
Bishop	Mr Lord

Canon	Canon
Cardinal	Your Eminence
Chief Rabbi	Chief Rabbi
Lord High Commissioner	Your Grace
Moderator	Moderator
Monsignor	Monsignor XXX
The Pope	Your Holiness
Prebendary	Prebendary
Priest	Father XXX
Provincial	Father Provincial
Provost	Mr Provost or Provost
Rabbi	Rabbi XXX
Vicar or Rector	Mr XXX or Father XXX

In the case of a vicar or rector, *never* refer to the Reverend XXX or Reverend XXX. However, the addresses of 'the Reverend Mr XXX' or, less formally, 'the Vicar' or 'the Rector' are acceptable.

Legal titles

Circuit Court Judge	Judge XXX
Court of Appeal Judge	Lord Justice XXX
High Court Judge	Mr/Mrs Justice XXX
Lord Chancellor	My Lord Chancellor
Lord Chief Justice	My Lord Chief Justice
Lords of Appeal	Lord XXX
Master of the Rolls	My Lord Master of the Rolls
Queen's Counsel	Mr/Mrs XXX

Diplomatic and Civil Service titles

All Civil Service appointments	By names, not appointments
Ambassador	Your Excellency
Charge d'Affaires	Charge d'Affaires, or by name
High Commissioner	High Commissioner, or by name
Minister	Minister, or by name

Academic titles

Chancellor of a university	Mr/Madam Chancellor
Vice-chancellor	Mr/Madam Vice-chancellor

Lesser titles can be embraced in the catch-all 'My Lords, Ladies and Gentleman'.

Of course, many organisations have their own forms of address, which you should do your best to master if you are unfamiliar with them.

In general, detailed formality in subsequent references to lesser titles can be dispensed with nowadays, though it is best to check beforehand whether offence would be given if the biggish wig were not shown sufficient deference throughout your speech.

Appendix 3
After Dinner Jokes and Stories

This appendix provides a miscellany of jokes and humourous stories, all of which can be adapted and personalised to suit the special circumstances and bring in the personalities who are at the dinner.

In choosing any particular joke for retelling at a function, the first consideration should be suitability. Firstly, is it in good taste, bearing in mind the type of audience to be present? Secondly, does it relate to the theme of the speech? If the answer to both these questions is yes, then it could well enhance your speech.

JOKES ABOUT JOBS

The theme that unites many audiences relates to their shared occupation. So here are some jokes about jobs.

Accountants

The personnel department of (name of company) had carefully interviewed 23 people for the job of assistant to the financial director. The chief executive (or name him) thought that one candidate – (character) – seemed ideal. He had been to a major public school. Not only was he a qualified accountant, but he also had five years experience in (nature of business) and had just been awarded a master's degree in business administration. ('Character'), said the chief executive, 'we'd like to offer you the job. And as you're so well qualified and experienced we've decided to start you off on a slightly higher salary than the one advertised. We'll pay you £60,000 a year.' 'Thank you,' replied (character). 'But how much is that per month?'

Advertising

(Character) used to work for (advertising agency) and he had to find a new advertising gimmick for a tea manufacturer. He decided to go with his secretary to Rome to see if he could persuade the Pope to make a TV commercial. The Pope gave him an audience and (character) made his request. 'We'll give you one hundred thousand pounds for a ten second ad. All you have to say is "Give us this day our daily tea".'

'I'm sorry,' replied the Pope, 'but I cannot do as you request.' 'Five hundred thousand' offered (character). 'I'm afraid not,' said the Pope, solemnly. 'All right, one million pounds. And that's my last offer.' But the Pope refused to make the commercial and (character) left. On the way home he turned to his secretary and said, 'That's odd. I mean, the Pope refusing to do a commercial for tea. I wonder how much the bread people are giving him?'

Armed services
My old grandpa had an exciting life though. During the War he served with Monty in the desert, and he told me that whenever they went into action, Monty always used to ask him to fetch his red tunic. After this happened, my grandpa asked Monty why he did this, and Monty said, 'It's quite simple – if I'm wounded in action, and the troops see I'm wounded, they might lose heart, the will to win. Can't have that. Not playing the game. But with my red tunic on the blood is less likely to show.'

Just then four dispatch riders drew up with reports to say that 5,000 of the enemy were approaching the rear, 10,000 were advancing dead ahead, 15,000 on the right flank and 20,000 on the left flank – simultaneously. Without batting an eyelid Monty turned to my old grandpa and said, 'Fetch my brown trousers.'

Building site
When (character) was interviewed for the job, his supervisor asked, 'Can you make tea?' (character) said, 'Yes'. 'And can you drive a fork lift truck?' his boss continued. 'Why,' asked (character), 'how big is the teapot?'

Buyers
(Character) would never accept a bribe. One day he was offered a Porsche. He was indignant. 'I cannot accept a gift like that,' he fumed. 'I quite understand,' replied the would-be briber, 'I tell you what, why don't I sell it to you for a fiver?' (Character) thought about it for a moment and then said, 'In that case, I'll take two.'

Car dealers
(Character) pointed to an old Escort. 'I can't shift this,' he said,
'I'll have to reduce it.' 'By how much?' I asked. 'Oh, by three
owners and 50,000 miles,' he said.

Chemists
I went into this chemist. There was a woman behind the counter –
there always is when I want anything personal . . . I've got more
tubes of toothpaste and bottles of Lucozade than Boots . . .
anyway, I was determined not to be put off – didn't want to spoil
my weekend – so I said to this frosty-faced woman behind the
counter, 'Three packets of thingies, miss.' She said, 'Don't you
miss me!' So I said, 'All right – four packets of thingies!'

Commercial travellers
I broke down in the middle of Salisbury Plain. A filthy night, it
was, all snow and ice, but as luck would have it, I'd broken down
just outside an old farmhouse. So I banged on the door and asked
if I could stay the night. The old farmer said, 'Well, we've got just
two bedrooms – one for the wife and me and one for our daughter
– but you're welcome to doss down on the sofa.' At about four
o'clock in the morning, the farmer's wife appeared and said, 'I'm
very worried about you being warm enough.' She said, 'Would
you like our eiderdown?' I said, 'Don't worry love – she's been
down twice already!'

Doctors
There were three women in (character's) waiting-room with their
daughters. When he saw them he went up the wall. (Character)
said to the first woman, 'It's no use you coming to see me again.
I've told you your trouble – you smoke too much. You're besotted
with the weed – you've even called your daughter after a tobacco:
you called her Virginia.' Then he said to the second woman, 'And
I don't want you wasting my time, either. I've told you your
trouble – you drink too much. You even called you daughter after
alcohol: you called her Sherry.' And the third woman stood up
and said, 'Come along Fanny, I haven't come here to be insulted.'

Fire-fighters
I went on this shout and there was this beautiful blonde trapped in
a third floor room. I shinned up my little ladder, jumped into the
room and said, 'You're alright now, don't worry.' She wasn't

wearing much – just a film of smoke – and she said, 'Oh, thank goodness you've come!' I said, 'You know, it's a funny thing, but you're the second pregnant girl I've rescued this year.' She said, 'But I'm not pregnant!' I said, 'You're not rescued yet!'

Florists
When I left school I worked in a florist's, but I got the sack. I had to put the labels on the flowers, and I got them all mixed up – very embarrassing. The flowers going to a wedding I put a funeral card on, and it read, 'With deepest sympathy.' And the flowers for a funeral, I put a wedding card on, and it read, 'Hope you'll be happy in your new home . . .'

Inland Revenue
A frantic-looking woman came rushing out of her house into the street and cried, 'Help! Help! My young son has just swallowed a coin and is choking. I don't know what to do!' The people in the street all looked the other way, except one (general description of character, like 'middle-aged man') who rushed into the woman's house, found her young son, turned him upside down and shook him violently until the coin fell out of his mouth. 'Oh, thank you!' cried the woman in happiness. 'Are you a doctor?' 'No, madam,' (character) replied. 'I'm with the Inland Revenue.'

Journalists
When (character) was a junior reporter with (local newspaper), the editor asked him, 'Did you get that story about the man who sings bass and tenor at the same time?' 'There's no story in it, sir,' replied (character). 'The man has two heads.'

Lawyers/barristers
(Character) faced the female witness and asked, 'Is it true that you committed adultery on the 3rd of February, in a snowstorm, while riding on the roof of a hearse travelling at 100 miles an hour through (local town), with a chorister from Canterbury Cathedral who was waving a Union Jack and singing *Football's Coming Home?*' The young woman in the witness box looked straight at (character), and said, calmly, 'What was that date again?'

Police
Before (character) joined us at (police station) he was a community copper in (local village). It was one in the morning when

(character) received a phone call from an elderly man. 'I can't sleep for the noise,' he complained. 'What's causing it? Do you want me to make an arrest or seize their music equipment?' (character) asked. 'I don't know. It's two cats mating on the wall outside my house. They're making a hideous racket with all their love-making and things.' 'Cats!' exclaimed (character). 'Why don't you walk up to the cats, give one of them a sharp prod and tell it that he is wanted on the phone?' 'Will that stop them?' the old man asked. 'Well it certainly stopped me,' (character) replied bitterly.

Teachers
A young lad asked (character), 'Sir, can I be punished for something I haven't done?' 'Of course not,' (character) replied. 'That's good,' he said, 'cos I haven't done my homework.'

HUMOUR ABOUT HOBBIES

If it's some leisure activity that brings them together, then that is what you should be talking about.

Amateur dramatics
Apart from *that*, Mrs Lincoln, how did you enjoy the play?

A friend of mine desperately wanted to be a famous actor and always believed in trying to 'live' the characters he portrayed. When he was invited to audition for the part of Abraham Lincoln, he found out as much as he could about the old president. He researched Lincoln's background for weeks, perfected an American accent and even dressed exactly like him – black top hat, long black coat, large black boots, the lot. After admiring himself in a mirror he set off for the audition. He didn't get the part – but while he was in the theatre he was assassinated.

Boxing
This old insomniac boxer was allergic to sleeping pills. The doctor said, 'The old remedies are the best. Just relax and start counting to a thousand.' The aged pugilist was back in the surgery within a week. He said, 'It's no good, doc. I keep jumping up at the count of nine.'

Cinema

(Character) was sitting in (local cinema) watching (current film) when a very fat lady got up during the interval and stepped painfully on his toes while squeezing past into the aisle. A short time later, the same fat lady returned, carrying an ice cream and a large packet of popcorn. 'Did I step on your toes?' she asked. 'I'm afraid you did. And you didn't apologise.' 'Good,' snapped the woman. 'Then this *is* my row.'

Competitions

I'm very competitive, me! I didn't get home till three in the morning the other night. The wife was furious! 'Where have you been?' she said. 'I've been in the pub with the lads.' She said, 'Till three in the morning!?' I said, 'Yes.' She said, 'And what's that you've got under your arm?' I said, 'It's a duck.' She said, 'I can see it's a duck. Where'd you get it?' I said, 'Down the pub, with the lads. We had a sort of – er . . . er . . . competition, like. And I won. This is my prize.' 'What sort of competition?' I said, 'Well . . . er, we were making . . . comparisons, like . . . our manliness, if you see what I mean . . .' She said, 'You've been showing to the whole world everything that's dearest between us, have you?' I said, 'No, love – just enough to win the duck . . .'

Cricket

I took the dog out for a walk the other Saturday afternoon, through the woods, and suddenly he starts barking like crazy at something on the grass under the trees. So I went over and there's a cricket ball. Old Fido, he goes on a bit and then starts barking away again – and there's another cricket ball a-lying on the ground. We walked on a few yards – and what do you think Fido found next? . . . A cricket crying its eyes out.

Cycling/driving

I drove here this evening. I was doing 65 down the (local motorway) when this cyclist overtook me – a cyclist! Pedalling like mad, he was. I thought that's a bit odd, so I pushed up my motor to 70 and overtook him. Couple of minutes later he went past me again – whoom! His little legs belting up and down so fast you could hardly see 'em. Eat your heart out Chris Boardman, I thought. But I just couldn't get my head around this so – naughty I know – I put my foot down till I whizzed past him at 80! Whoom! Would you believe it – zoom! – he came past me again. I began to think I was seeing things so at the next slip road I turned off the motor-way to have a think. There was a tap on my window – it was the cyclist. I opened the window, and he said, 'Thank God you've stopped, I've got my braces caught in your back bumper!'

Football
I make donations to (name of local club) each season. I put a one pound coin in an envelope and sent it off last year. I got a very nice letter back from the Chairman saying 'Thank you for the pound you sent. Which two players do you want?'

Golf
A veteran golfer I know at (name of local club) was constantly defeated by the 16th hole. That hole always got the better of him, always made him finish one or two strokes over par. He told his wife, 'When I die, I want to get my own back on that 16th hole if it kills me! Promise me you'll have my ashes scattered all over that damned hole.' And sure enough, when he died, after the funeral, his wife solemnly scattered his ashes all over the 16th fairway – and the wind blew them out of bounds.

Swimming
I learned to swim at a very early age. When I was three my parents used to row me out to sea in a little boat until they got about a mile from the shore – then I had to swim back. I quite liked the swim – it was getting out of the bag that was difficult.

Tennis
(Character) practises by hitting a tennis ball against his garage door. He hasn't won yet, but last week he took the door to five sets.

Theatre
A friend of mine has a pet duck he takes everywhere with him. Last week my pal was most upset because, although he bought two tickets, the duck was refused admission to the theatre. So he decided to stuff the duck down his trousers and pretend to be a little overweight. The ruse worked, and my friend got in to see the show. Everything went well until the intermission when the duck got very hot and poked his beak out of my friend's trousers, through the flies. Two old ladies were sitting next to my friend and one nudged the other and whispered 'Look at this.' The other lady said, 'I can't stop looking at it – it's eating my ice cream!'

Appendix 4
Apt and Amusing Quotations

Everyone enjoys hearing a particularly witty turn of phrase or apt quotation during an after dinner speech. Below are some that could help your speech along. To remain in tone with the rest of the book, I have avoided anything remotely sentimental or profound and instead concentrated on the whimsical, light-hearted and entertaining.

None of these quotable quotes will be received with a knee-slapping belly laugh. Their merit lies in their encapsulation of a truth, a smart observation or a humorous example. They are intended to promote smiles and nods rather than helpless mirth. For this reason, they should be spread thinly, like caviar, not piled on liberally like marmalade. Two or three quotes on a given theme are plenty enough for any after dinner speech.

After dinner speaking
An after dinner speech should be like a lady's dress – long enough to cover the subject and short enough to be interesting (Rab Butler).

As the mother whale said to her young 'Remember, my dears, you can only be harpooned when you're spouting' (Anon).

'Stand up to be seen, speak up to be heard, shut up to be appreciated' (Anon).

Age
The gardener's rule applies to youth and age: When young, sow wild oats; but when old, grow sage (H. J. Byron).

You know you're getting old when the candles cost more than the cake (Bob Hope).

Age is a question of mind over matter. If you don't mind, it doesn't matter (Dan Ingman).

Babies
People who say they sleep like a baby usually don't have one (Leo J. Burke).

Now why did you name your baby 'John'? Every Tom, Dick and Harry is named 'John' (Sam Goldwyn).

A perfect example of minority rule is a baby in the house (Anon).

Cricket
I ran for a catch
With the sun in my eyes, sir . . .
Now I wear a black patch
And a nose such a size, sir! (Coulson Kernahan).

My father was one of the few umpires of my experience who appealed along with the bowler (Michael Parkinson).

The first ball he received he lashed at wildly and hit it straight up in the air to an enormous height . . . Up and up it went and then at the top it seemed to hang motionless in the air poised like a hawk, fighting, as it were, a heroic but forlorn battle against the chief invention of Sir Isaac Newton (A. G. Macdonald).

Drinking
I'm only a beer teetotaller, not a champagne teetotaller (George Bernard Shaw).

The Swiss love to pour a little cognac into everything . . . At a dinner I attended in Lausanne an Englishman tasted so much brandy in the soup that he lifted his plate of consomme\'e and declared solemnly: 'Ladies and Gentlemen – the Queen!' (George Mikes).

The wine flowed like water, towards the end of the evening it tasted like it (Spike Milligan).

Education
A primary duty of education is to let curiosity rip (Ivor Brown).

We were involved in the Herculean task of discovering how long it would take six men to build a wall if three of them took a week. I seem to recall we spent almost as much time on this problem as the men spent on the wall (Gerald Durrell).

Nothing worth knowing can be taught (Oscar Wilde).

Foreign travel
Continental breakfasts are very sparse, usually just a pot of coffee or tea and a teensy roll that looks like a suitcase handle. My advice is to go right on to lunch without pausing (Miss Piggy).

In an underdeveloped country don't drink the water, in a developed country, don't breathe the air (Jonathan Raban).

I dislike feeling at home when I am abroad (George Bernard Shaw).

Gambling
The race is not always to the swift, nor the battle to the strong – but that's the way to bet (Damon Runyon).

Never bet on anything that can talk (John McCririck).

I backed the right horse, but the wrong one went on and won (Henry Arthur Jones and Henry Herman).

Law
On the whole, barristers are more interested in their briefs than in a girl's (Jilly Cooper).

To appeal, in law, is to put the dice back in the box for another throw (Ambrose Bierce).

Laws, like houses, lean on one another (Edmund Burke).

Life
Life is rather like a tin of sardines. We are all looking for the key (Alan Bennett).

Life was always like this. Just as something nice and interesting occurred, destiny must intervene with some pressing engagement (Conrad Aiken).

Life is a steady walk with a hidden precipice at the end (Lambert Jeffries).

Money
That money talks
I'll not deny.
I heard it once –
It said 'Goodbye' (Richard Armour).

A gift shop in Yorkshire has a sign which says: 'Credit given only to customers over 85 – accompanied by both parents!' (*The Daily Telegraph*).

Money nowadays seems to be produced with a natural homing instinct for the Treasury (The Duke of Edinburgh).

Music
Tenors are noble, pure, and heroic, and get the soprano. But baritones are born villains (Leonard Warren).

My friends tell me that my rendering of a Scarlatti sonata sounds best from the garden (Wynford Vaughan-Thomas).

Brass bands are all very well in their place – outside and several miles away (Thomas Beecham).

Politeness
They say courtesy costs nothing, but it's surprising how many people can't seem to afford it (J. Basil Boothroyd).

I beg your pardon for calling on you in this informal way, but your house is on fire (Mark Twain).

A gentleman is a man who gets up to open the door for his wife to bring the coal in (Anon).

Politics
We all know that politicians are wedded to the truth, but like other married couples, they sometimes live apart (Saki).

As a politician never believes what he says, he is surprised when others believe him (Charles de Gaulle).

The whole art of political speech is to put *nothing* into it. It is much more difficult than it sounds (Hilaire Belloc).

Success
Success makes people, for the most part, humble, tolerant and kind. Failure makes people bitter and cruel (W. Somerset Maugham).

The toughest thing about success is that you've got to keep on being a success (Irving Berlin).

Failures are the steps that lead to success. Success is the blind alley at the top of the steps (Lambert Jeffries).

Glossary

Adapting. Changing material so it better meets your needs.

Anecdote. A short personal story.

Anniversary hook/closer. Beginning or ending a speech by reference to anniversaries that fall on this day.

Articulation. A way to form sounds.

Booster. A short gag within another joke or story.

Bombing. Being unsuccessful.

Bracketing. Planting words or images at the start of the speech and returning to them at the close.

Bridging. A transition from one subject to another – see **Linking**.

Bummer. A joke that **bombs**.

Closers. Those vital final words of a speech – see **Hooking**.

Corpsing. Either forgetting your words, or laughing uncontrollably.

Dead-spot. The time when laughs or audience reaction has abated but another line has yet to be delivered.

Enunciation. Emphasising key words, syllables and phrases.

Exaggeration. A type of joke (see page 27).

Eye contact. Maintaining direct visual contact with members of the audience.

Feedback. The reaction that the audience gives to the speaker.

Fluffing. Stumbling over your words.

Gesture clusters. A series of body language gestures which collectively give out a consistent silent message about a person's emotions or attitudes.

Hooking (an audience). Making an audience sit up and listen – see **Closers**.

Humour hook/closer. Beginning or ending a speech with humour.

Illogical logic. A type of joke (see page 27).

Insult. A type of joke (see page 27).

Lighthouse technique. A method of maintaining **eye contact** with the entire audience.

Linking. Keeping jokes and ideas on the same subject flowing – see **Bridging**.

Modulation. Varying pitch and tone.

One-liner. A short joke, though not necessarily of just one line.

Pay-off/sting/punch line/tagline. The culminating part of a joke that gives it its point.

Personalising. Naming characters, locations, etc. known to an audience in jokes and stories.

Picture. A type of joke (see page 27).

Pitch. Degree of acuteness of a sound.

Positioning the pay-off. Placing the key word or words of a joke where it or they are likely to receive the maximum reaction.

Projection. Art of making one's voice heard at distance by the use of good breathing and muscle control rather than shouting.

Pun. A type of joke (see page 27).

Question hook/closer. Beginning or ending a speech with a question.

Redundancy. Intentionally repeating yourself to aid comprehension.

Rehearsal. Practising your speech.

Reverse. A type of joke (see page 27).

Rhythm. The choice and combination of words that can become music to an audience's ears.

Set-up. The beginning of a joke which sets the context and lays the groundwork necessary before the **punch line** can be delivered.

Structuring/routining. Arranging material in a logical order so it will glide smoothly, like a narrative.

Switching. Taking the idea behind a funny but unrelated joke and transferring it to the subject and theme of your speech.

Theme. A speech's one main idea.

Timing. Regulation of actions or remarks to produce the best effect.

Topper. A joke that uses an earlier gag as its **set-up**.

Transitions. Words that link ideas.

Truthfulness. A type of joke (see page 27).

Twisted cliché. A type of joke (see page 27).

Word play. A type of joke (see page 27).

Working an audience. Delivering a speech in the way that is most appropriate for any particular audience.

Further Reading

PUBLIC SPEAKING

The Complete Public Speaker, Gyles Brandreth (Robert Hale).
Janner's Complete Speechmaker, Grenville Janner (Business Books).
Just Say a Few Words, Bob Monkhouse (Arrow).
Making a Wedding Speech, John Bowden (How To Books).
Making the Best Man's Speech, John Bowden (Essentials).
Making the Bridegroom's Speech, John Bowden (Essentials).
Making the Father of the Bride's Speech, John Bowden (Essentials).
Mastering Public Speaking, Anne Nicholls (How To Books).
Mitch Murray's Handbook for the Terrified Speaker (Foulsham).
Powerful Business Speeches, John Bowden (How To Books).
Speaking in Public, John Bowden (Essentials).

ANNIVERSARIES

The Amazing Almanac, Gyles Brandreth (Pelham Books).
The Anniversary Book, Christopher Downing (Futura).
The Book of Days, Anthony Frewin (Collins).
Chambers Dates (Chambers).
Hamlyn Dictionary of Dates and Anniversaries (Hamlyn).
On This Day: The history of the world in 366 days, Sian Facer (Hamlyn).
Today's the Day, Jeremy Beadle (W. H. Allen).

QUOTATIONS

The library shelves are weighed down with these books. I find the following particularly useful:

A Dictionary of Contemporary Quotations (David & Charles).
Apt and Amusing Quotations, G. F. Lamb (Elliot Right Way Books).

Cassell's Book of Humorous Quotations (Cassell).

The Dictionary of Twentieth Century Quotations, Nigel Rees (Fontana).

The Guinness Dictionary of Quotations for all Occasions, Gareth Sharpe (Guinness Publishing).

The New Penguin Dictionary of Quotations (Viking).

The Oxford Dictionary of Modern Quotations (OUP).

The Oxford Book of Quotations (OUP).

The Penguin Dictionary of Humorous Quotations, Fred Metcalf (Viking).

Stevenson's Book of Quotations (Cassell).

ANECDOTES AND JOKES

There are hundreds, perhaps thousands, of these books. Here is a personal selection:

The Faber Book of Anecdotes, Clifton Fadiman (Faber).

Jokes and Quotes for Speeches, Peter Eldin (Ward Lock).

One Liners for Business, Mitch Murray (Foulsham).

One Liners for Speeches on Special Occasions, Mitch Murray (Foulsham).

One Liners for Weddings, Mitch Murray (Foulsham).

The Public Speaker's Joke Book, Kevin Goldstein-Jackson, (Elliott Right Way Books).

The Right Joke for the Right Occasion, Kevin Goldstein-Jackson (Elliott Right Way Books).

1497 Jokes, Stories and Anecdotes, Herbert V. Prochnow (Sterling).

3500 Good Jokes for Speakers, Gerald Lieberman (Thorsons).

MISCELLANEOUS

Body Language, Michael Pease (Positive Paperbacks).

The Power of Your Subconscious Mind, Joseph Murphy (Simon & Schuster).

Simple Relaxation, Laura Mitchell (John Murray).

Use Your Head, Tony Buzan (BBC/Open University).

Visual Thinking, Rudolph Arnheim (Faber).

Visualisation, Ursula Markham (Element Books).

Voice and the Actor, Cicely Berry (Virgin).

Useful Addresses

The following lists are far from exhaustive. They include organisations which I can personally recommend, or which have been personally recommended to me.

SPEECH TRAINERS

Ivor Spencer Enterprises Limited, 12 Little Bornes, Dulwich, London SE21 8SE. Tel: (0208) 675585/(0208) 6708424. Fax: (0208) 6700055. e-mail: ivor@ivorspencer.com

Speakers Corner, 94 Albury Drive, Pinner, Middlesex HA5 3RF. Tel: (0208) 8688967. Fax: (0208) 8684409. e-mail: speakers@agents.uk.com

Straight Talking, 15b Abingdon Road, London W8 6AH. Tel: (0207) 9381080. Fax: (0207) 937758. e-mail: mail@straight-talking.ndirect.co.uk

SPEAKERS' AGENCIES

Celebrity Speakers Limited, Eton Place, Burnham, Buckinghamshire SL1 7JT. Tel: (0173) 747400. Fax: (0173) 747401. e-mail: csi@speakers.co.uk. web: www.speakers.co.uk

International Artistes Limited, Mezzanine Floor, 235 Regent Street, London W1R 8AX. Tel: (0207) 4398401. Fax: (0207) 4092070. e-mail: (user)@intartistes.demon.co.uk

Interphiz Ltd, 4 Kew Green, Richmond, Surrey TW9 3BH. Tel: (0208) 9400007. Fax: (0208) 9400007. e-mail: performers@interphiz.com. web: http://www.interphiz.com

INTERNET

The Internet changes so rapidly that any listing here would be obsolete within a week. However, major search engines can be used to find a wide range of speaking topics, ranging from speech trainers and speakers' agencies to books and cassettes. For the amateur speaker, the Internet is also valuable, appropriately enough, for its many 'chat' rooms and support groups.

Index